SKY TALES

MORE INSIGHTS FROM A LIFE IN THE SKIES

CAPTAIN LIM KHOY HING

© 2017 Lim Khoy Hing

Photographs © Lim Khoy Hing, unless otherwise specified
Illustrations © Straight to Point Advertising

Published by Marshall Cavendish Editions
An imprint of Marshall Cavendish International (Asia) Pte Ltd
1 New Industrial Road, Singapore 536196

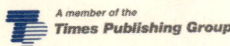

All rights reserved

No part of this publication may be reproduced, stored in a retrieval system or transmitted, in any form or by any means, electronic, mechanical, photocopying, recording or otherwise, without the prior permission of the copyright owner. Requests for permission should be addressed to the Publisher, Marshall Cavendish International (Asia) Private Limited, 1 New Industrial Road, Singapore 536196. Tel: (65) 6213 9300. E-mail: genref@sg.marshallcavendish.com
Website: www.marshallcavendish.com/genref

The publisher makes no representation or warranties with respect to the contents of this book, and specifically disclaims any implied warranties or merchantability or fitness for any particular purpose, and shall in no event be liable for any loss of profit or any other commercial damage, including but not limited to special, incidental, consequential, or other damages.

All illustrations in this book are used in jest. Scenes and events depicted are in no way representative of AirAsia's code of conduct, business operations, or staff behaviour.

Other Marshall Cavendish Offices:
Marshall Cavendish Corporation. 99 White Plains Road, Tarrytown NY 10591-9001, USA • Marshall Cavendish International (Thailand) Co Ltd. 253 Asoke, 12th Flr, Sukhumvit 21 Road, Klongtoey Nua, Wattana, Bangkok 10110, Thailand • Marshall Cavendish (Malaysia) Sdn Bhd, Times Subang, Lot 46, Subang Hi-Tech Industrial Park, Batu Tiga, 40000 Shah Alam, Selangor Darul Ehsan, Malaysia

Marshall Cavendish is a registered trademark of Times Publishing Limited

National Library Board, Singapore Cataloguing-in-Publication Data

Names: Lim, Khoy Hing. | AirAsia, publisher.
Title: Sky tales : more insights from a life in the skies / Captain Lim Khoy Hing.
Description: Singapore : Marshall Cavendish Editions ; [Malaysia] : Air Asia, [2017]
Identifiers: OCN 990164846 | 978-981-47-7923-4 (paperback)
Subjects: LCSH: Flight. | Aeronautics. | Flight crews.
Classification: DDC 629.1325--dc23

Printed in Malaysia by Vivar Printing Sdn Bhd
Lot 25, Rawang Integrated Industrial Park
Mukim Rawang, off Jalan Batu Arang
48000 Rawang, Selangor

This book is dedicated to my wife, Koh Hui Ching;
my daughter and son-in-law, Lim Pei Mun and Jeff Shotton;
my son and daughter-in-law, Lim Kok Chian and Vivian Chok;
and my grandchildren,
Alex, Marcus, Annabelle, Yi Yin and Hao Vern

CONTENTS

FOREWORD		7
ACKNOWLEDGEMENTS		9

PART ONE – SAFETY AND MYTHS

Chapter 1:	Miracle on the Hudson	14
Chapter 2:	Safer in the Sky	21
Chapter 3:	No Fears, No Tears	27
Chapter 4:	Busting Aviation Myths	34

PART TWO – FLYING THE PLANE

Chapter 5:	Navigating the Blue Skies	42
Chapter 6:	Gravity Matters	47
Chapter 7:	Weighty Matters	53
Chapter 8:	Passenger Etiquette	59
Chapter 9:	On Top of the World	67
Chapter 10:	Out of the Cockpit	73
Chapter 11:	Stowaway Woes	77
Chapter 12:	Wrong Landing Strip, Captain!	82
Chapter 13:	Going Around	88
Chapter 14:	Cockpit Challenges	95
Chapter 15:	Safe Snaps	101
Chapter 16:	Have a Pleasant Flight	108

PART THREE – FLIGHT CREW

Chapter 17:	Saluting the Cabin Crew	118
Chapter 18:	An Aviator's Ascent	126
Chapter 19:	Ally in the Skies	131
Chapter 20:	A Pilot's Life	136

PART FOUR – HEALTH AND MEDICAL ISSUES

Chapter 21:	The Dry Dilemma	144
Chapter 22:	Easy, not Queasy	149
Chapter 23:	Fight the Fatigue	154
Chapter 24:	Sleeping on the Job	159
Chapter 25:	Fit to Fly	165
Chapter 26:	Red, Green or White	171
Chapter 27:	Coping with Jet Lag	177
Chapter 28:	Travel Bumps	183

PART FIVE – PLANES AND HARDWARE

Chapter 29:	Travellers' Quests	190
Chapter 30:	Planes and Fuels – Sharklets to the Rescue	199
Chapter 31:	Machine versus Man	207
Chapter 32:	The Glass Cockpit	213
Chapter 33:	Blows and Birds	220
Chapter 34:	Secret Revealed	226

PART SIX – WEATHER

Chapter 35:	Weathering Obstacles	236
Chapter 36:	Bumps in the Air	242
Chapter 37:	Winds Beneath Your Wings	246

DOWN MEMORY LANE	256
ABOUT THE AUTHOR	266

Tony Fernandes
AirAsia Group CEO

FOREWORD

I remember when Captain Lim first approached me in February 2012 to do a book. He had been writing a monthly column on flying for AirAsia's inflight magazine, *Travel 3Sixty*, for four years then, and he felt he had enough material to compile into a single volume.

He first volunteered to pen the column, *Pilot's Perspective*, after noticing there were no articles about flying in the magazine, and because he felt it was important to demystify the flying experience for our guests. You could say the column was an extension of his personal blog, in which he aimed to shed light on various aspects of air travel, especially for the benefit of first-time flyers.

Captain Lim's commitment to making flying more enjoyable for everyone is laudable, so when he asked if I would sponsor his first book, I immediately said yes. He has a wealth of experience from decades of being a commercial pilot, and I believed a wider audience would benefit from his expertise and knack for explaining even the most complicated things in a way everyone can understand.

That first book, *Life in the Skies*, was a modest success, with 18,000 copies sold since October 2013, and more than 3,000 copies of the Chinese edition sold since July 2015. It was placed third in the POPULAR–*The Star* Readers' Choice Awards at Bookfest @ Malaysia 2015 (English, Non-Fiction category).

More importantly, the book has brought comfort to countless readers who, armed with a greater understanding of what happens before, during and after every flight, have been able to overcome their fear of flying.

Since then, Captain Lim has continued to inform and entertain with new columns — enough to compile into a second book, which is what you hold in your hands. His tireless dedication is the reason I could not be more thrilled or honoured to write a foreword for this book, in which Captain Lim continues to do what he does best — share his passion and knowledge about flying with the world.

ACKNOWLEDGEMENTS

So I achieved my lifetime dream of writing a book that got published in 2013. With that, I should be enjoying my retirement by taking things easy, spending time with family and grandchildren, and travelling for leisure.

However, flying is my passion. It is my life, and I cannot stay away. I continue to work full-time as a ground school and flight simulator instructor with AirAsia X, as well as contribute to the airline's inflight magazine, *Travel 3Sixty*, and answer questions from curious and fearful flyers on my website, "Just About Flying".

This second book is a natural extension of all of the above, and it would not have been possible without the assistance of so many individuals.

I would like to express my deepest gratitude to Tan Sri Tony Fernandes for sponsoring this second book. Even though he is a busy man, he has never failed to show his humour, kindness and humility every time we meet. Once again, he has agreed to pen the Foreword.

Many thanks also to the managing editor of *Travel 3Sixty*,

Beverley Rodrigues, for her very professional editing, and internal editor Yow Hong Chieh for fine-tuning this book and Alex Tsen for the wonderful illustrations. I would also like to name the following for making this book possible. Thank you Datuk Kamarudin Meranun, Executive Chairman AirAsia Bhd, Bo Lingam, COO AirAsia Group, Aireen Omar, CEO AirAsia Bhd, Benyamin Ismail, CEO AirAsia X Bhd, Siegtraund Teh, Spencer Lee, Jesslyne Heng, Rudy Khaw, Sumeet Dhingra, Nurdiyana, Jonathan Lee, Glenn Wray, Christine Chong, and the *Travel 3Sixty* team comprising R. Rajendra, Chitra Santhi Nathan, Kan Seak Hong, Shamini Sugananthan and Fazlina Bee Abdul Rashid for helping to make this book a success. I am also very grateful to many others who have, in one way or another, been involved in this endeavour.

With more than 45 years of flying experience and many million air miles under my belt, I have had the pleasure of flying in various aircraft — as a pilot, and as a passenger. I am hopeful that this second book will give you a better glimpse of my flying history, with pictures from the days of black-and-white and sepia-tone photography, to the more colourful, recent shots.

During my search for historical planes from the archives, I found out that a current colleague of mine, Sri Ramani Kugathasan, isn't "just" a licensed aircraft engineer; he is also an avid plane spotter with a large collection of plane photographs. My special thanks to him for kindly allowing me to use some of the photos from his album.

I would also like to thank the following, who have given me permission to use their personal or airplane images: Captain Noor Hafizah, First Officer Jessica Lee, Captain Chanaporn Rosjan, Teerawut, Joop de Groot and Ken Fielding. Special thanks to Ariff Shah for the front and back cover photos, and Alex Chia, AirAsia Creative and 123RF.com for the images inside the book.

I am also very grateful to my daughter, Lim Pei Mun, who still enjoys helping to proofread my articles regularly, and making sure I don't overcomplicate things so that they can be enjoyed by everyone.

With that, I hope you all will enjoy reading this book.

Safe flight always!

Captain Lim Khoy Hing

PART ONE
SAFETY AND MYTHS

Chapter 1

MIRACLE ON THE HUDSON

What's the likelihood of surviving a water landing during an emergency? This is a question that pops up in my inbox frequently. Well, the 2016 movie, *Sully*, which depicts the famed "Miracle on the Hudson", shows how it is possible to emerge safely from such an unfortunate event. The movie, directed by Hollywood legend Clint Eastwood and starring Tom Hanks as Captain Chesley "Sully" Sullenburger, dramatises the US Airways Flight 1549 crash of 2009, in which all 155 passengers and crew on board were saved after a bird strike.

The Airbus A320 piloted by Captain Sully and First Officer Jeffrey Skiles was on a domestic flight from LaGuardia Airport in New York to Charlotte Douglas International Airport in North Carolina. Three minutes after taking off, the plane struck a flock of Canada geese at 3,000 feet, causing both the engines to lose power immediately.

Are pilots trained to handle two-engine failures? Yes. However, most flying practice focuses on only one engine getting knocked out during the take-off. To have two engines

A US Airways Airbus A320 with New York in the background.

fail once airborne is extremely rare. Dual-engine failure training is normally conducted at very high altitudes to show the distance a plane can glide without propulsion.

For instance, if dual-engine failure occurs at 40,000 feet, a plane can glide about 100 miles and stay in the air for 15 minutes easily. That would allow the pilot and crew sufficient time to prepare for a safe emergency landing.

In the Hudson River incident, both engines failed at a very low altitude, leaving Captain Sully and his co-pilot only about three minutes to decide what to do. When the birds struck the engines and the plane immediately began to lose height, Captain Sully first attempted to turn back to LaGuardia. He was also advised to land at another nearby airport, Teterboro, in New Jersey. Unfortunately, he realised that both options were not within the gliding range of the plane.

When I used to fly to New York City, I would land at Newark International Airport, to the south of Teterboro Airport. Hence I'm quite familiar with its location when approaching from the north, and am reminded of how daunting it would be to handle an emergency in such a congested environment.

Newark International Airport was my favourite destination during my flying days. It is about 15 miles southwest of Midtown Manhattan and was the first major airport in the United States. Up until 2013, it was also the busiest in the area in terms of flights.

In 2015, Newark handled 37.5 million passengers; John F. Kennedy (JFK) International Airport handled 56.8 million, and LaGuardia, 28.4 million. Combined, these three airports in the New York metropolitan area made up the largest airport system in the US and the largest in the world in terms of total flight operations.

As such, traffic within this airspace is always very busy. I always found it difficult to find a pause in between the streaming radio communications in order to pass a message to the air traffic controllers. The native New Yorkers would speak very quickly, and because the traffic was so busy, it could be quite awhile before you were acknowledged and notified of the landing sequence. This can be especially stressful when your plane's approach to the runway is imminent. It was always such a relief when they finally called through. The best policy, I learned, was to be patient while the controllers were busy talking with the other pilots and say nothing until they called. It was certainly stressful!

Fortunately, during an emergency, the plane affected is always given top priority. When Captain Sully informed air traffic control (ATC) of his predicament, he was given immediate assistance. Teterboro was suggested, but he declined and opted to glide over the Hudson River as the safest course of action.

He eventually ditched the plane off a point near the Intrepid Sea, Air & Space Museum. This museum has the fascinating SR-71 Blackbird parked on the deck of the USS Intrepid, an old aircraft carrier built during World War II for the US Navy.

THE SR-71 BLACKBIRD

I was rather intrigued by this plane and remember walking all the way from the Radisson Martinique on Broadway at 32nd Street, a block from the Empire State Building, to 46th Street just to see it.

The Blackbird was renowned as the Cold War spy plane. During aerial reconnaissance missions, it operated at very high speeds and altitudes, which allowed it to outrace any threat. If a surface-to-air missile launch was detected, the standard evasive action was simply to accelerate and outfly the missile!

The SR-71 Blackbird.

The SR-71 was used by the US Air Force from 1964 to 1998. A total of 32 aircraft were built; 12 were lost in accidents, but none to enemy action. This plane was developed after the US Air Force U-2 spy plane was shot down by the Soviet Union in 1960, in its airspace.

Some trivia about the Blackbird: It was designed to cruise at just over three times the speed of sound or more than 2,200 miles per hour (Mach 3.2), at altitudes up to 85,000 feet. The plane looked more like a spaceship than an aircraft and 90% of it was made of titanium to withstand extreme temperatures when flying at very high speeds.

The Blackbird was able to avoid being detected by radar because it was painted with a black paint filled with radar-absorbing iron. The US did not produce titanium, but it was able to acquire the ore through third parties from the Soviet Union. So, it was the 'enemy' that contributed to the success of this super spy plane.

THE AIRBUS DITCHING BUTTON

Back to Captain Sully and the spectacular water landing. The Airbus A320 has a ditching button to close all the valves located underneath the aircraft, to prevent flooding during a ditching. However, in the Hudson River incident, the flight crew, in the heat of the moment, did not activate the switch.

Captain Sully later noted that it probably would not have been effective anyway as the force of the water impact tore holes in the plane's fuselage that were much larger than the openings sealed by the switch. He also noted that the impact could have been less violent, but was prevented from getting maximum lift manually during the crucial four seconds before the plane hit the water. This was because the software within the controls is specifically designed to prevent the plane from pitching down at low speed for safety reasons.

Questions continue to be asked about overall air safety. If you measure the number of crashes against the overall amount of aviation traffic, 2016 was one of the safest years in recent aviation history.

"We are ahead of the 10-year average with eight accidents and 167 fatalities compared to the average of 10 accidents and 205 fatalities," Geoffrey Thomas, an aviation expert and editor of Airlineratings.com, said in a CNN report dated May 20, 2016.

According to data released by the International Air Transport Association, in 2015, more than 3.5 billion people flew safely on 37.6 million flights (31.4 million by jet and 6.2 million by turboprop).

As for commercial airlines, there is no other form of transportation that is so thoroughly investigated and monitored to enhance air safety. Arnold Barnett, a professor of statistics in the Massachusetts Institute of Technology (MIT), said the fatality risk per flight in the US was one in seven million.

You may say statistics do not allay your fear of flying and think that perhaps travelling by train would be safer. I hope the facts will help you reconsider.

According to rail accident records over the past 20 years, the chances of dying on a transcontinental train journey are one in a million, compared with one in seven million on a plane. And, according to figures from the Natural History Museum of Los Angeles County, the odds of dying from a bee sting are higher than in a commercial flight crash!

Chapter 2
SAFER IN THE SKY

With strict regulations governing the aviation industry, flying is one of the safest modes of transport out there today.

You may have heard the joke about pilots who, upon landing, would announce to their passengers: "The safest part of your journey is now over." This is no idle boast or sweeping statement.

I can safely say that you face more risks going home on the road than on a flight, for two simple reasons. It's easier to get

Flying is one of the safest modes of transport.

a driving licence than a pilot's licence, and the maintenance of motor vehicles is less stringent compared with the strict regulations imposed on jetliners and pilots.

This is not to say there are no procedures governing ground transportation. But should a car catch fire on the road, the driver can stop the vehicle and get out. Pilots and their passengers do not have that luxury.

Therefore, the airline industry insists that for planes to be certified fit for the carriage of passengers, they must be far safer than any ground vehicle.

AVOIDING FIRES AND COLLISIONS

In the extremely remote event of an engine fire, there are two special fire extinguishers affixed to each aircraft engine. There are also fire extinguishers in the cabin should a fire start on board. Pilots are trained to handle fire drills in flight simulators and to react promptly should a fire warning be activated.

Emergency responses include shutting down the correct engine and activating the fire extinguisher. Through continuous training, these responses are perfected to ensure that fires or other emergencies will be handled deftly and safely. Fabrics and seat cushions in the airplane cabin are all fire-retardant and tested to ensure they do not emit toxic fumes. Should smoke be detected within the cabin, emergency lights will come on along the cabin floor to guide passengers to the nearest emergency exit for safe evacuation once the plane lands. Such safety features are unlikely to be found in most modes of ground public transport.

A plane's structural strength must also meet incredibly high safety standards before it can be declared safe. For instance, plane seats are designed to withstand 16 times the force of gravity.

When a Boeing 777 crash-landed at the San Francisco Airport on July 6, 2013, its main structure and seats were sturdy enough to protect almost all the passengers from the impact.

Today, we also have the traffic anti-collision avoidance system, which helps ensure that planes do not collide in the air. If two planes are on a collision course, computers on board will alert the pilots with commands such as, "Climb, Climb!" or "Descend, Descend!"

The pilot will immediately use his flight instruments to fly the plane and stay within the green band, which is the safe zone, until it is clear of danger. A "Clear of Conflict!" notification will be issued once the plane has safely avoided the approaching aircraft. Subsequently, the pilot will submit a report of the "near-miss" to the ATC. Investigations will then be carried out to determine why the danger arose and what measures should be taken to ensure that the skies are safer in the future.

SAFETY FEATURES

Can modern aircraft fly upside down? Although one often sees planes doing that in Hollywood movies or at air shows, this is not possible with modern commercial jetliners because their physical controls do not allow them to fly beyond a particular position.

There is also another safety feature that ensures a plane does not stall or lose lift in the wings in the air. If onboard computers sense that a plane is on the verge of stalling, the automatic power system or thrust levers will kick in to prevent it from falling from the sky. It must be stressed that all these safety features can only function properly if, and only if, all the computers are operative. In Airbus aircraft, for example the A330, there are five flight control computers to ensure that the plane is controllable in any emergency situation. Compare that with the absence of any computers in an average car on the ground.

Statistics from the Malaysian Institute of Road Safety Research show that in 2016, there were 19 road fatalities per day, or about 7,150 a year, in the country, which had a population of 31.7 million then. If there were some form of ground traffic anti-collision avoidance system, it would be a major step towards reducing accidents on the roads.

A RELIABLE VEHICLE

In the United States, 2012 was one of the safest years for commercial aviation: The fatality rate for airline passengers was one in 45 million flights. According to Prof Barnett of MIT, flying has become so reliable that a traveller in the US could fly every day for an average of 123,000 years before being involved in an airplane crash!

Believe it or not, the fact is that planes and engines have become more and more reliable. Advanced warning technology has sharply reduced once-common accidents such as mid-air collisions or aircraft crashing into mountainous terrain in adverse weather.

In-flight briefings enhance the safety and welfare of passengers.

The grounding in 2013 of the Boeing 787 Dreamliner fleet after the fire issue with its lithium battery illustrates the precautionary measures taken by the industry. The last time a fleet — the DC-10 — was grounded was in 1979, after a McDonnell Douglas DC-10 crashed shortly after take-off from Chicago O'Hare International Airport, killing all the 271 people on board as well as two on the ground.

Chapter 3
NO FEARS, NO TEARS

When I was a kid, my parents never had to worry about me and my siblings when it came to air travel. It was never going to happen as we were too poor to even afford a bus ride!

I took my first flight at 19, when the Royal Military College that I was attending visited a flying school in the north of Malaysia. We flew on a propeller plane, a twin-engine eight-seater de Havilland Dove. I was not fearful of flying; instead, I was looking forward to it.

Many children love flying and air travel.

However, many children and adults suffer from aerophobia, or the fear of flying. Children do not usually know how to deal with it and may cry or scream, misbehave by attempting to stand on their seats or even try to remove their seat belts. To help them overcome aerophobia, parents first need to learn more about flying so they can show their children what they can do.

EASING AIRPLANE EAR

A blocked ear canal may cause pain at altitude. Sounds like a simple thing, doesn't it? But this minor problem can become the root of a lifetime of fear and angst.

My granddaughter became fearful of flying after suffering excruciating pain from a blocked ear during descent. After that, she refused to fly anywhere. I gradually explained to her that it was her blocked ear that had caused the pain. An imbalance of air pressure caused by a blocked eustachian tube had stretched the sensitive membrane in her ear.

To reduce the risk of this happening, avoid flying with children if they have a severe cold. Sometimes, when a child has a mild cold or a sinus problem, her ears can become blocked. You can suck on a sweet or blow against a pinched nose and closed mouth (called the Valsalva manoeuvre) to clear the blockage. Alternatively, try moving the jaw from left to right a few times. This will usually push air into

Anatomy of the Ear

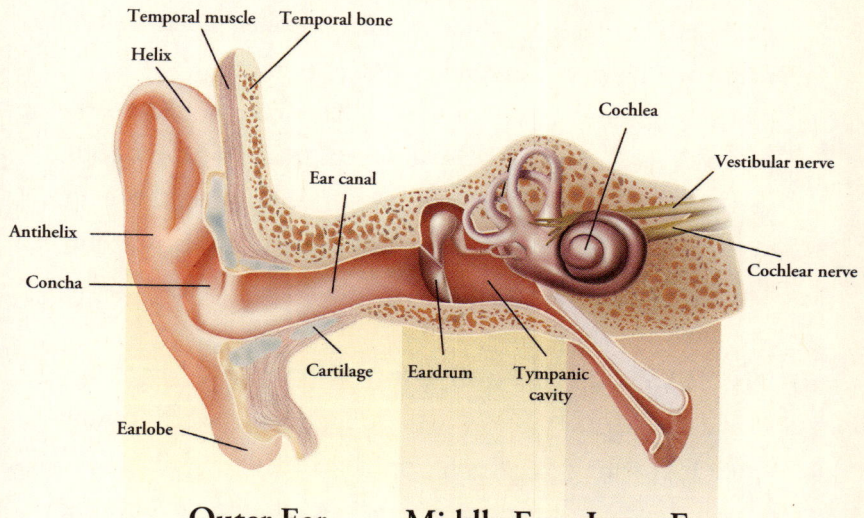

A blocked ear canal (eustachian tube) may cause pain during a plane's ascent or descent.

the middle ear, thereby equalising the pressure and easing the pain.

My granddaughter is especially prone to airplane ear because her eustachian tube is narrower than normal. This often causes it to be blocked, which results in air not being able to travel up to the middle ear. Blockages are usually caused by mucus and inflammation as a result of a cold or throat infection. She understands the situation better now and knows how to blow her ears to clear her eustachian tube.

A family doctor might be able to help by prescribing antihistamine tablets, which should be taken a day before flying, to reduce the amount of mucus produced.

Decongestant tablets or syrups have been found to be useful. A nasal spray can dry up mucus in the nose too. Kid-sized external air pressure regulating earplugs can also help as they slow the rate of air pressure change on the eardrum. Ideally, these should be worn before the aircraft door is closed.

THINGS THAT GO BUMP ON BOARD

A plane in flight produces some strange noises which can be quite frightening to a young child. As such, explaining the various noises in the cabin before take-off and while flying will help reduce her anxiety.

For instance, the clunking noise just after a plane is airborne or before landing is the sound of the wheels going up or down. The roar of the engines as a plane rumbles down the runway can be deafening and may need explanation to ease unnecessary fear.

On the ground, there will be background hum from equipment that supplies electricity, as well as air conditioning for the cabin. The modern jet engine takes a while to start and during this process, the lights will flicker and other pieces of electrical equipment can be heard stopping or starting.

Soon after the landing flaps have been selected, the

noise of the screw jack kicks in, and the transfer unit of the hydraulic pumps in an Airbus A320 creates a sound that could be mistaken for a dog barking inside the cargo hold!

When the plane is taxiing, expect a thumping noise as its nose wheel passes over taxi lights. A frequent air traveller will treat all these noises as routine, but not a child. After take-off, the sound of the engine will change to a lower pitch as the power settings are reduced. This is normally associated with a sinking feeling during the power-reduction process, when the pilot pulls back the power and slows the rate of climb.

A child's fear may be further compounded by the reduction of the engine noise, which can make her believe that something is wrong with the engines.

During the landing phase, the thrust reversers add to the noise level, but all these noises are perfectly normal. Knowledge of this will enable adults to explain any abnormal sounds or motions to a child.

UNDERSTANDING TURBULENCE

A modern aircraft can take up to at least 150% of the strongest force it could possibly meet in flight, and is therefore not really affected by turbulence. However, a shaking plane may upset an anxious child who does not understand what is going on.

Turbulence is a natural phenomenon in the air. It is more prevalent around jet streams caused by the Earth's rotation. Flying inside a jet stream is basically smooth. However, when flying in the vicinity of one, friction between fast-moving jet streams turns nearby slow-moving air into "ball bearings" of air.

When a plane is flying in these rolling ball bearings of air, passengers can expect a rough ride. Flying near a thunderstorm and through wind shear and unevenly heated air mass can produce similar effects. Therefore, sound knowledge of turbulence will enable an adult to confidently explain the often scary sensations to a child in a reassuring manner.

PREPARE FOR FLIGHT

Talk to your child about what will happen on the flight while on the ground. It may be useful to go into details about the noises to expect while boarding and during take-off and landing so that the strange or loud sounds do not come as a complete surprise.

If your child is frightened, crying loudly, struggling to get out of her seat or refusing to buckle up, calm her down with a hug and reassure her that everything will be fine. Most kids do eventually calm down, unless something is physically troubling them, such as a blocked ear.

LET THE LIGHT IN

These days, my grandchildren are far less fearful of flying as they have the benefit of a pilot grandfather to help them understand the mechanics of flight. For others who do not have such an advantage, learning about aircraft and the issues involved in flying is a good idea.

Being able to explain the troubling sounds and sensations children might experience will go a long way towards easing their anxieties and fears, and help them enjoy the amazing experience of travelling across the world by air. As Ralph Waldo Emerson said, "Knowledge is the antidote to fear".

Chapter 4
BUSTING AVIATION MYTHS

There are people who believe everything they hear, treating every story they come across as truth. Always remember: The movies would be quite boring if they showed the mundane realities of life.

Stories are told and retold with exaggerations in order to hook an audience. Action and drama sell tickets, whereas the truth doesn't.

SHOOT-OUTS AND SUCTION

In the 1964 spy film *Goldfinger*, British secret agent James Bond shoots at the window of a small airplane and the villain is sucked out across the cabin. In another movie, the bad guy shoots out an aircraft door, causing every passenger and bag to be sucked out of the plane through the hole.

I was once asked by a curious traveller if that could really happen on a plane. The truth? A small hole caused by a gunshot like that in the Bond film would not have become larger. If such an incident happened in real life, a safety (outflow) valve that controls pressurisation in the

The movies tend to perpetuate aviation myths to hook viewers.

plane would automatically close to reduce the rapid loss of cabin pressure.

However, larger holes do create strong suction, as happened on Aloha Airlines Flight 243 in 1988, when a section of the overhead cabin roof blew off owing to metal fatigue. Fortunately, the passengers were all strapped in and survived the explosive decompression. But there was one fatality: A flight attendant was swept overboard during the decompression.

QUICK GETAWAYS IN THE SKY

In movies, quick getaways in an airliner appear to be as easy as if one were just jumping into a car and speeding away. This is far from the truth. For instance, before a pilot can start flying an Airbus A330, both he and the first officer have to run through at least 140 checks: 90 following the "Before Engine Start" checklist and another 50 prior to taking off.

Unlike the driver of a car who probably goes through only four steps before heading off — open the door, buckle up, turn on the ignition switch and step on the accelerator — an airline captain has to brief the crew and check through everything first as he shoulders a very heavy responsibility: the lives of hundreds of passengers.

For instance, the captain will compare his altimeter with that of the first officer to ensure that all the instruments are in good working condition. Both pilots also have to check the engine oil to ensure the quantity is sufficient for the journey.

As such, the cockpit crew has to be in their respective positions at least 45 minutes before take-off to carry out all these checks meticulously.

DRAMATIC AERIAL STUNTS

In the movie *Flight 2012*, there was a lot of drama when the captain, played by Denzel Washington, ended up flying inverted during an emergency. But he was able to right the plane again before crash-landing it — an almost impossible feat in a real commercial aircraft.

In reality, the aviation industry has a well-structured set of procedures on handling an emergency, following this exact order: aviate, navigate, communicate and manage. Training following the golden rules of flying ensures that an emergency is safely handled with as little drama as possible, just as Captain Sully did.

When asked in an interview whether he prayed just before crashing into the Hudson, he said he believed his passengers were doing that for him. His priority was to bring the plane down safely, just as he had been trained to do.

DROPPING OXYGEN LEVELS

Some people believe that oxygen levels decrease as altitude increases. This is a fallacy. The percentage of oxygen at higher altitudes is about the same as that at sea level — 21%. What changes is air pressure, which drops as altitude goes up. At sea level, the air pressure is 14.7 pounds per square inch, or about one kilogram per square centimetre. This makes it easy for the oxygenated air we breathe in to pass into our bloodstream.

The oxygen level at 10,000 feet is still the same as that at sea level, but the air pressure is 30% lower because the air is less dense. As air molecules become increasingly dispersed at higher altitudes, each breath we take delivers less oxygen to the body. So, at 10,000 feet, you're breathing in about 30% less oxygen than at sea level! Hence, cabin pressurisation is very important to maintain air pressure as a plane flies higher.

TOILET TRAUMA

Then there is this movie myth that has been going around and scaring first-time travellers: If you flush an airplane toilet while sitting down, your bottom can get sucked in.

While it is true that the force of the plane's toilet suction system is strong, you would probably only get stuck if your body forms a perfect seal on the toilet seat. However, it is still a good idea to raise your bum a little or stand up before flushing.

FEMALE PILOTS

The stereotypical view is that airline pilots need to be all-rounders who are physically fit and have great spatial awareness. This is true to a certain extent, but it also suggests that only men embody such traits.

Views on gender roles in society have evolved and the glass ceiling is being smashed daily, enabling women to move up, head multinational companies and excel in what was once bastions of male dominance.

The airline industry is no different — it is slowly attracting more and more members of the fairer sex. Today, AirAsia has the largest number of female pilots in the country.

AirAsia X A330 Captain Noor Hafizah is one of the female captains in the airline.

All pilots are thoroughly tested for their performance in safety and decision-making skills and no special considerations are given to anyone. As such, guests who fly with AirAsia are assured that only the best are piloting the aircraft, regardless of their gender.

FACT VERSUS FICTION

While stories and movies can be quite entertaining, it does help to separate fact from fiction so that you can have peace of mind when flying. I hope these facts on flying will make you a happier and better-informed air traveller!

PART TWO
FLYING THE PLANE

Chapter 5

NAVIGATING THE BLUE SKIES

How does a pilot navigate in what looks like an empty sky? Even though the sky may look empty from the ground, it is a web of many invisible airways. Indeed, a flight from, say, Kuala Lumpur to London traverses many routes or airways. Unlike highways where motorists can rely on signboards and exit markers, the skies have no road signs. As such, pilots are trained to navigate from point A to point B from the day they start learning to fly.

In fact, "navigate" is one part of the first golden rule in the aviator's mantra: aviate, navigate, communicate and manage. In aviation terms, to navigate basically means to plan the course of a plane by using flight instruments or maps.

A pilot does not need to remember the airway he is flying in as he can refer to airway charts and use a flight management computer. Here, I will explain the various navigation techniques, from the very basic to more advanced forms.

AT ITS MOST BASIC

From day one, a pilot trainee is taught the basics of navigation: recognising ground landmarks such as buildings, rivers, shorelines, mountains, etc. This is typically mastered in flying clubs or schools that use smaller planes. Note that such basic navigation is only good for flying in perfect weather, at low altitudes and for short distances.

RECKONING ONE'S POSITION

The next basic means of navigation is to calculate a plane's position based on its known speed and direction. For example, if you know your position from 10 minutes earlier and you know that you have travelled due west at 480 knots (or eight nautical miles a minute), simple calculation will show that you are now 80 nautical miles west of your previous position.

This, in air navigation terms, is known as dead reckoning. It requires an accurate fix or position of where the plane is, in what particular direction it is heading, and at what speed. (Mathematics is a mandatory subject that one must excel in to qualify as an airline pilot.) As the pilot progresses to more advanced flying in bigger planes, at higher altitudes and for longer distances, navigation by other means becomes necessary.

NAVIGATING BY RADIO

Radio navigation works by picking up signals from a transmitter on the ground. When a plane is tuned to the frequency of a particular airport station down below, a pointer or dial on the instrument panel in the cockpit will home in on that station. So, in that sense, navigation from the air is easy — just fly towards the station!

But this technique of homing a plane in on a particular point or airfield following radio signals is susceptible to weather interference, which can affect navigation. A more reliable radio navigation aid is the Very High Frequency Omnidirectional Range (VOR) beacon, which transmits stronger and more accurate signals from the ground. VOR stations are often located with a Distance Measuring Equipment (DME) transmitter and, together, they enable a pilot to know exactly how far the aircraft is from the station.

In that sense, when he is within a maximum range of 250 to 300 nautical miles, the pilot is always able to determine the plane's location.

INERTIAL NAVIGATION

If you understand the principle of dead reckoning, then inertial navigation is easy to comprehend. While the former requires the human brain to compute the position of a plane, the latter is performed automatically by a system of gyroscopes.

Put simply, inertial navigation uses three sensitive gyroscopes to measure changes in speed in three directions. The changes are then used to calculate the speed and position of the plane.

Inertial navigation is used in larger planes. Like dead reckoning, it requires an accurate fix or position. However, this system has since been replaced by the even more accurate global positioning system (GPS), similar to those used in your car, such as Garmin, or by the ubiquitous apps on the smartphone, like Waze.

GLOBAL POSITIONING SYSTEM

In aviation worldwide, the GPS has been further refined to provide very accurate guides that enable planes to land in difficult terrain. Using GPS, airplanes can now manoeuvre between canyons and make precise turns onto a runway without seeing more than just clouds. The GPS guides the plane to safely break out of clouds and aligns it straight on the centre line of a runway. But such approaches can only be flown by aircraft equipped with GPS systems that have been certified to a certain level of accuracy. The pilots must also be specially trained to fly with such navigational aids.

Chapter 6
GRAVITY MATTERS

What makes apples fall from the tree? What stops you from floating off into space? Gravity — the force that pulls or attracts a body towards the centre of the Earth.

Tightrope walkers understand this better than anyone else. Precariously navigating a rope that seems as fine as a thread with just a balancing pole as an aid, these stunt artists are able to entertain us because they understand the simple concept of the centre of gravity (CG).

On a plane, this concept is equally important. A conventional aircraft normally has a forward CG. It is designed in such a way that should anything happen to the engines, the nose of the aircraft would dip downwards, allowing the plane to glide.

Most planes glide well. For example, an Airbus A330 can glide without engines for about 160 kilometres from a height of 40,000 feet! This was proven when, in 2001, Air Transat Flight 236 ran out of fuel owing to a ruptured fuel line en route from Toronto, Canada, to Lisbon, Portugal. The pilots made history by flying the plane without power and gliding to a safe landing on an island in the Azores region in the Atlantic Ocean.

SEATS FOR A SMOOTH RIDE

The position of the CG is very important, in terms of safety as well as helping the airline save costs and be competitive. As a passenger, you would not know where the position of the CG is, but a rough guide would place its safe range as somewhere near the wings.

The front of the plane is usually quieter and this is where the first- or premium-class seats are located. Equally comfortable are the seats near to the CG because they would be the least affected by turbulence. A passenger who is prone to air sickness should choose seats as close to the wings as possible.

Think of the plane as a see-saw, where the centre is placed on a pivot called the fulcrum. The farther away one is from the fulcrum, the more motion one would experience. This is where turbulence tends to be amplified. Just like in a bus, the bumpier seats are those at the back.

Technically, the CG of the plane moves around the centre of the wings and not exactly in the middle of the cabin. The CG also changes as the fuel is consumed. So, any seats near or just forward of the wings would provide a smoother ride than anywhere else.

NOSE- OR TAIL-HEAVY — WHICH IS BETTER?

Did you know that where you sit on the plane is determined by a qualified and licensed professional called a dispatcher or loadmaster? This person is responsible for planning the way a plane is loaded. He calculates weight and plans cargo and passenger placement to keep the aircraft within the permissible limits of its CG throughout the flight.

At times, depending on the weight of its cargo and the number of passengers on board, a plane may be either nose- or tail-heavy, but always within the safe range as stipulated by aviation regulations.

A forward CG is nose-heavy, which means more force is required to raise the nose when taking off. It has more drag (opposing force), which affects fuel consumption. An aft

CG (slightly tail-heavy) plane gives better cruise speed and controllability.

For any medium-range Airbus A320 or A330 aircraft, the preferred CG position would be at the rear, as the flight controls for the pilot are lighter. Prior to take-off, the pilot will inspect the load sheet to ensure the CG is within the safe limit and in the optimum position for the particular flight.

During the landing phase, the pilot aims for the rear wheels to touch the ground first, followed by the nose wheels. Hence, a slight aft CG would be more desirable. However, in a less-than-perfect landing, especially with a forward CG, the nose wheel may touch the ground earlier than usual with a thump at the front, but that is a fairly infrequent occurrence.

WEIGHT AND BALANCE

As you can imagine, the weight and distribution of passengers on board the plane is a significant factor to ensure a smooth flight. Most airlines use a standard weight of 75kg for an adult passenger, but there are several factors that may alter this figure.

For example, on a flight departing from Kuala Lumpur for Melbourne during winter, a loadmaster must take into consideration the weight of the average Caucasian passenger, which is usually heavier than that of the average Asian passenger, as well as the fact that passengers may be carrying thick jackets to prepare for the chilly weather upon landing. AirAsia X usually allocates 80kg per Caucasian passenger.

For passengers who have not pre-booked their seats, the loadmaster will distribute seating to ensure a well-balanced cabin. On a light flight, passengers have a tendency to move around, opting for seats other than their assigned ones. This could affect the weight and balance of the aircraft. Sometimes, when the CG is too far forward, the captain will ask the crew to move passengers from the forward cabin to the back of the plane.

NO SEAT-HOPPING!

As a passenger, you can definitely do your part to help your favourite airline maintain a smooth flight by not unnecessarily altering the position of its CG, especially when you move away from your assigned seat or congregate at the back of the plane for a casual group chat.

On smaller or lighter planes, ensure that your cabin bags are not overloaded. A small airliner operating out of a Chicago airport once had a close call. The captain reported that he needed more power and a longer distance to lift off the runway than what he had initially expected.

Upon investigation, it was found that most of the passengers on board were coin collectors who were travelling to a convention with more than a ton of coins in their carry-on baggage!

Remember that you will be charged excess baggage fees if you overload your check-in bags. Some airlines also impose a weight limit on each piece of luggage to ensure that ramp agents are not overly taxed when lifting them. Some baggage handlers have refused to accept very heavy luggage, owing to the high rate of back injury, a hazard of the profession.

So, if you thought that only people struggle with their weight, think again — airliners do too. However, airline weight issues cannot be remedied by following the latest diet fad.

It takes the cooperation of a lot of people to ensure balanced weight distribution for a smooth flight.

Chapter 7
WEIGHTY MATTERS

One of the major challenges to overcome when flying is the problem of weight (or gravity). The Greek myth about Icarus' doomed flight attempt comes to mind. Icarus was able to overcome gravity by flying with wings made of wax and feather. But he defied his father's order not to fly too near to the sun and, as a result, his wings melted and he fell into the sea.

In an airplane, the weight problem is overcome by lift, which is generated by the shape of the wings. Air flowing on the upper surface of the wings has a lower pressure than at the bottom (Bernoulli's theorem), resulting in lift. (Newton's laws on motion also explain how an aircraft gets lift, but I will not deal with that here.)

WEIGHT AND BALANCE

An aircraft commander is responsible for the safe loading of the plane and he must ensure that it is not overloaded as that has serious safety and economic implications. An overloaded plane takes a longer time to get airborne, which means it requires a lengthier runway. The climbing rate would be reduced, hence lowering the optimum ceiling and affecting the flight range. It consumes more fuel too. Furthermore, an overweight plane will be adversely affected structurally during landing.

WEIGHT AND THE CONCORDE

Weight plays a very important part in flight safety. In fact, the tragic crash which led to the demise of the Concorde, the world's first supersonic commercial plane, was partly blamed on the aircraft being overweight when it took off.

On July 25, 2000, an Air France Concorde flying from Paris to New York plunged to the ground minutes after take-off, killing all 109 aboard and four people on the ground. According to the accident investigation report, the plane ran over a strip of metal on the runway and burst a tyre. A chunk of rubber hit the fuel tank inside the wing, causing the jet fuel to pour out and set fire to the wings.

This might not have happened if the plane had not been overweight by six tons. Why? If the plane had been lighter, it would have become airborne before it could run over the metal strip.

DO AIRPLANES HAVE WEIGHING SCALES ON THE LANDING GEAR?

The weight of a plane is important as the pilot must not take off if it is above the designed weight. It does not generally have a system akin to the weighing scale on the landing gears but has a similar mechanism as an option, mostly found on cargo planes. However, these are uncommon and not widely used because they are unreliable. The normal practice of calculating the actual take-off weight is based on computation by the dispatchers.

HOW IS THE WEIGHT MEASURED?

The basic weight of a plane is normally calculated in the factory. However over time, an aircraft's weight can change mainly owing to accumulation of moisture, dust, dirt or modifications. For example, a new coat of paint on a Boeing 747 weighs eight to nine tons! Thus, to keep track of weight growth, planes have to be weighed every two to three years.

Aircraft weighing is usually carried out by certified companies. One way of weighing the plane is to jack it up on stands at three or more points. Load cells are fitted in between the jacks to provide the weight information as well as the CG position.

An airplane with a forward CG is more stable. In fact this is one of the requirements during certification from a safety point of view. For instance, at a higher cruising altitude, the forward CG will induce the nose to drop so that the plane will naturally recover from a stalled condition, just like a paper plane.

WHY DO PLANES DUMP FUEL?

Every commercial plane has a certified maximum landing weight. For example, the MLW of an Airbus A320 is 66 tons. For the A330 and A340, it is 187 tons and 192 tons, respectively. Only the four-engine Airbus A340 operates over a long range and consumes a considerable amount of fuel. Hence, its landing weight is very much less upon landing than at take-off (275 tons).

During an emergency, the A340 has a fuel jettison facility to get rid of excess fuel in order to land below the MLW. On average, it can dump one ton of fuel per minute. For example, if I were to take off at 202 tons and an emergency arises, I will have to dump 10 tons of fuel over 10 minutes to land at the regulated MLW of 192 tons.

Dumping fuel is expensive but landing overweight can be just as costly. Aircraft can, and do, land overweight in some emergencies.

Only bigger planes such as the A340 and some A330 have dumping facilities. Smaller planes like the Airbus A320 do not need such a system because of their lighter weights and shorter range.

TO DUMP OR NOT TO DUMP?

The US Federal Aviation Administration has come up with guidelines to help a captain to come to a decision

Image by Sri Ramani Kugathasan

An Airbus A340 has a fuel jettisoning system.

should he be worried about damaging the environment. To land overweight (hence no dumping) in the event of a malfunction, the pilot must be certain the malfunction will render the plane unsafe if he were to waste more time jettisoning fuel. Furthermore, he should not dump but land immediately if there is a passenger who is seriously ill and requires immediate medical attention.

Environmental studies have shown that, in general, fuel jettisoned above 5,000 to 6,000 feet will completely vaporise before reaching the ground. Therefore, the general recommendation is to dump fuel above that altitude whenever possible. However, there is no restriction on jettisoning at lower altitudes if it is considered necessary in an extreme emergency.

A pilot can still land overweight without dumping fuel, but the plane will need to undergo maintenance inspection after that. The engineers will look for obvious signs of damage caused such as wrinkled fuselage skin, popped fasteners or bent components. If overstressing is found, a more detailed inspection is required to examine critical structural components before the plane is allowed to fly again.

I hope that knowing about weight and its impact on flying will help passengers understand its importance in contributing to a safe flight. Well, this is a gentle reminder to all our guests to not carry any overweight hand luggage!

Chapter 8
PASSENGER ETIQUETTE

It's interesting how good manners can oftentimes completely disappear when patience wears thin and tempers fray in a less-than-ideal situation.

I've observed this at the departure gate when, frustrated by a slight delay, passengers jostle to board the plane and claim space in the overhead cabin before anyone else can take up the choice spots.

I recently received an email from a traveller regarding a less-than-fragrant aroma in the cabin as a result of outside food being smuggled on board. Unfortunately, neither the guest nor cabin crew could track down its source, so the guest (and all those around her) had to endure the odour as best they could.

As a pilot who takes the welfare and comfort of my guests seriously, I really felt for this guest. I'm not always a captain on duty, tucked away in my comfortable cockpit. Often, I travel as a passenger and I, too, have been in her place and experienced frustration and annoyances.

Therefore, sympathising with this fellow traveller — who

could very well be a passenger under my care — I shall tackle the issue of airplane etiquette.

MOST ANNOYING HABITS

Interestingly, travel expert Expedia compiled a list of the most annoying habits of airplane passengers in its 2015 Airplane Etiquette study.

Lack of thoughtfulness and consideration towards fellow travellers is one of the key factors that fan annoying passenger behaviour. But, who do you think tops the list?

According to Expedia, the top spot goes to rear seat kickers — usually young children who repeatedly kick, prod or tap the seat in front of theirs with feet or knees — who seem oblivious to the fact that their actions can cause the entire row before them to reverberate with an unwelcome rhythm.

If you're unfortunate enough to encounter a seat kicker, simply turn around and politely ask if he would mind stopping what he is doing. Smile as you talk to the youngster or adult offender. This usually works, for a while at least. If a reminder is required, be sure to deliver it with a tight smile and a stern look that show you mean business.

NOISY KIDS

Second on the list are inattentive parents allowing their children to run wild within the confines of the cabin. As a parent, I know how trying it is to keep active children quiet when they're bursting with energy and itching to run about.

And then, of course, there are the screaming babies. I sympathise with tired parents travelling with young children. I'm sure they need to rest just as much as the other passengers.

JetBlue, a low-cost airline in the US, came up with a rather innovative idea of turning the crying of babies into something positive. Ingeniously, JetBlue offered a 25% discount to every passenger every time a baby started crying. To enjoy a completely free flight, a passenger would have to be inconvenienced by four fussy crying babies! According to the promotion, if one was "lucky" enough to have four little babies who disliked flying enough to let out a few awful wails during the flight, everyone on board would be entitled to free round-trip tickets on their next JetBlue flight.

This idea turned an annoyance into a desirable thing as passengers would cheer and clap every time a baby cried. Of course, the idea has a downside: Understandably, parents may feel embarrassed when all eyes turn their way. It is unclear whether JetBlue's promotion will become a popular feature, but it appears that the airline may not make it a regular thing.

I would suggest that parents carry card games, books or toys to entertain their young ones and stop them from running around the cabin. Babies are often bothered by the change in pressure, so always carry a pacifier for them to suck on to relieve pressure in the inner ear, a common cause of discomfort.

As for passengers who cannot abide the noise of crying babies, try asking a member of the crew if you could relocate to a quieter area of the cabin. If not, earplugs or headphones are a lifesaver!

PROTECTING PERSONAL SPACE
If you are unlucky enough to be seated between two passengers who are larger than yourself, you may not be

able to enjoy any elbow space on the shared armrest. This ranks quite high on the list of passenger grievances and is a tough one to handle. Both you and your seatmate have equal claim to part of the armrest. Should an inconsiderate neighbour claim all of it, my advice is to wait until he or she moves. Then immediately place your elbow on your share of the armrest. Be sure to tell your seatmate that you've left space for him or her so that the point — equal space — is clear.

Reclining seats, especially in airlines where the seats are much narrower, leaving less space between rows, can also cause discontent.

Many passengers actually recline their seat when the

passenger in front of them does so, causing a domino effect.

According to the Expedia study, some passengers think reclining seats should be banned entirely. Or, they should only be reclined during set times on short-haul flights. My take? Well, chairs are meant to be reclined for comfort, after the food is served. To overcome the inconvenience of having less legroom because your neighbour in front is reclining, simply join in. Alternatively, tilt your seat back slightly and relax.

CHATTY CATHY AND OTHER ANNOYANCES

While some passengers prefer peace and quiet, there are those who take the opportunity to meet new friends while travelling. Putting these two types next to each other is a recipe for frustration.

If you have a chatterbox as your seatmate, try yawning. If this subtle hint fails, have the courage to say, "Excuse me, I don't mean to be anti-social, but I'm going to try get some shut-eye for a while."

Then, of course, there are passengers who have a tendency to talk very loudly and continuously, and often over their seatmates, without a care as to whom they may be disturbing. You need to be direct with these. Smile, look into their eyes and say, "Excuse me, would you mind keeping your voice down?"

To me, the worst offenders of all are the boozy ones. Should you be seated beside a tipsy passenger, avoid eye contact as this may be interpreted as a sign of aggression. It's best to alert the cabin crew discreetly if they start becoming belligerent. Alternatively, request to be relocated before your tipsy seatmate passes out with his or her head on your shoulder or starts a fight!

ODOROUS PASSENGERS

If you are unfortunate enough to be seated with someone who removes his shoes, allowing his personal aroma to waft through the cabin, be brave and politely ask him to put his shoes back on as the smell is bothering you.

Or, if you dare, take off your own shoes and wiggle your toes at him! I'm just kidding, of course.

Basic courtesy dictates that your fellow passenger behaves in a considerate and hygienic manner and you are well within your rights to remind him or her of that. Just remember to be kind.

THE PERFECT PASSENGER

You can't control who you are seated next to… unless, of course, you and your friends or family book Hot Seats together when flying with AirAsia. However, you can control how you react to those who annoy. How you manage the situation could very well be the difference between an enjoyable flight and a hellish one.

Oftentimes, I believe people are just completely oblivious to what they're doing. I'd like to think that most of them are good-natured and would be willing to change when informed of an annoying habit.

Apparently, Japanese passengers are considered the world's best travellers because of their good manners and respect for others. Perhaps this graciousness is embedded in their culture. But with a bit of practice and thoughtfulness, anyone can be a polite passenger, ensuring an enjoyable flight for everyone on board.

Chapter 9

ON TOP OF THE WORLD

AirAsia X trains aircrew for charter flights to Xining airport, an airfield in China situated 7,165 feet above sea level. The airport at the highest altitude that the airline presently flies to is in Kathmandu, Nepal, and it is only 4,390 feet above sea level.

Xining, the capital of Qinghai province in western China and the largest city on the Tibetan Plateau, was a commercial hub along the northern Silk Road for more than 2,000 years and continues to be well known today. The city is now widely considered the perfect summer resort for locals and tourists alike, especially those visiting the Dongguan Grand Mosque, which showcases an exquisite blend of Chinese and Islamic architecture.

The mosque is one of Xining's main draws and has contributed to the gradual increase of air traffic in recent times. A similar shift is taking place around the world, where high-altitude destinations are gaining popularity in commercial air travel.

However, to operate in a high-elevation airfield such as

Xining, it is imperative that the flight crew is well-trained to handle the surroundings and circumstances that are unique to high-altitude flights.

There are various issues that a pilot must be aware of to ensure safe and efficient flight operations.

AIR AND SPACE

At higher elevations, a plane encounters lower air density. This affects the amount of lift generated by the wings and, subsequently, the aircraft's aerodynamic and engine performance.

One of the most noticeable effects of lower air density is the longer take-off run that airplanes require. The runways at high-altitude airports therefore need to be longer than usual. For instance, the longest runway at sea level is New York City's JFK International Airport, which is 14,511 feet. But the runway at Qamdo Bamda Airport in Tibet, China, located at an altitude of 14,219 feet, stretches some 18,045 feet. This airport was constructed to reduce travel time from the provincial capital, Chengdu, from two days by bus to about one hour by air.

Qamdo Bamda Airport was the highest airport in the world until it was superseded in 2013 by Daocheng Yading Airport, also in China. But Qamdo Bamdo remains home to the longest commercially-used paved runway in the world.

Syangboche Airport (12,402 feet above sea level), at Mount Everest National Park.

HIGH-ALTITUDE AIRPORTS AND HYPOXIA

It is important for aircrew to understand the effects of hypoxia to efficiently operate flights to high-elevation airports. Hypoxia is caused by insufficient oxygen supply to the body tissue and cells. Pilots are trained to recognise the symptoms that indicate the onset of subtle incapacitation (a stage whereby the crew are considered unfit to perform their flying duties), a result of hypoxia.

During my training days in the UK, every trainee was placed inside a decompression chamber to experience the effects of hypoxia and how it affects a pilot's performance. Inside this capsule-shaped chamber, the level of oxygen was reduced to simulate the effects of high altitude on the human body.

At first, before a climb to the desired altitude was simulated, we breathed oxygen from our oxygen masks so that nitrogen would be removed from our bloodstream. This was necessary to eliminate the possibility of decompression sickness, which can happen when sudden decompression sets off nitrogen bubbles in the body's tissues, causing muscle pain, nausea and even paralysis. The atmospheric pressure inside the chamber was then gradually reduced to simulate a high altitude and we were instructed to remove our oxygen masks so that we could experience the symptoms of hypoxia.

An aviation medical doctor, who retained his oxygen mask throughout the exercise, was present inside the chamber to place our masks back on in case any of the trainees passed out. There were also observers outside the chamber who monitored our responses to the simulation via closed-circuit television and viewing ports.

After we had removed our oxygen masks, the supervising doctor requested that we do simple arithmetic (addition and subtraction) and sign our name. I found the tasks easy to perform and was rather pleased with myself for completing everything effortlessly.

It was only after stepping out of the decompression chamber that we discovered, to our surprise, that the records kept by observers outside showed we had taken a prolonged amount of time to complete our menial tasks, and our signatures, which we thought were perfect, were merely scribbles! And all the while when we were inside the chamber, we had been totally unaware of this minor incapacitation.

So, not only did we blunder through the exercise, we also had the false impression that we performed well.

LOW ON OXYGEN

What happened? It turns out we had almost exceeded our time of useful consciousness (TUC) at that particular altitude. The TUC is the amount of time an individual is able to perform flying duties efficiently in an environment that has inadequate oxygen. Applying this to our decompression chamber exercise, it meant as we were exposed to an increasingly oxygen-deficient environment, our functioning capability decreased and we were no longer capable of taking appropriate corrective actions. For example, the TUC at 15,000 feet above sea level is about 30 minutes. At 35,000 feet, it is a mere 30 to 60 seconds! What's more, the TUC may decrease further if the individual is a smoker.

In an actual flight, this scenario is averted as the aircrew is trained to recognise the possible onset of hypoxia and to wear oxygen masks to avoid being affected, especially during an emergency descent.

TOPPING IT ALL

As more and more high-altitude destinations in the world become part and parcel of everyday air travel, the airline industry remains diligent in ensuring that all pilots are adequately trained and regulated for high-airport operations. The aim is not only to achieve the shortest possible travel time to the world's top high-altitude airports; it is also to guarantee an enjoyable, safe passage for passengers.

If you're a keen traveller, you should definitely put these "top of the world" airports on your must-visit list. A good idea would be to drop by Xining first to acclimatise yourself to high-altitude surroundings before setting off on an adventure to Qamdo Bamda or Daocheng Yading.

DID YOU KNOW?

World's highest airports
China has many scenic high-altitude airports. In fact, it has eight of the 10 highest airports in the world. Topping the list is Daocheng Yading, at 14,472 feet above sea level. The only two airports outside China on the top 10 list are El Alto International Airport (13,327 feet) in Bolivia (fifth place) and Inca Manco Cápac International Airport (12,552 feet) in Peru (seventh).

Chapter 10

OUT OF THE COCKPIT

Through my extensive travels both as a pilot and passenger, I have visited well-known destinations with modern airports and all the conveniences of city life.

One of the most basic needs of the modern traveller is a clean restroom at airports and while on tour. On a recent holiday to Inner Mongolia, I passed through three

Passengers transiting through a terminal want correct information on flight arrivals and departures.

international airports before arriving at a fairly remote destination. Our guide for the Mongolian grassland tour told the men in our group to "do it anywhere behind a bush" and the ladies to "use any open latrines in that shed" when we stopped for a break.

My group felt quite disenchanted as a clean restroom should be a basic requirement. Fortunately, the international airports in Kuala Lumpur, Guangzhou and Hohhot en route to our tour destination were clean, in contrast to the usual complaints of odour, no tissue paper and malfunctioning faucets at less-developed terminals.

EXPECTATIONS AND NECESSITIES

Also on a traveller's wish list would be correct information on flight arrivals and departures. This should be followed by a safe and comfortable place to rest before or between flights.

Indeed, our outbound journeys were highly satisfactory. I had expected Hohhot, the capital of Inner Mongolia, to be an old and remote airport in the grasslands, but it turned out to be modern and well-planned.

Guangzhou terminal is huge and very crowded and one member of my group went missing during the transit to Mongolia and again on the return journey. The limited English signage certainly made things a little disorientating for all concerned.

SECURITY AND IMMIGRATION

Security checks are very stringent in China. My mobile phone battery pack was confiscated even though it was packed in my check-in baggage as it did not have a label stating its battery capacity. This one was given to me as a gift when I bought my previous car. So, all smartphone users take note: If your smartphone battery-charging pack exceeds 20,000mAh, do not carry it into China, not even in your check-in bag.

In contrast, the experience of going through China's immigration was better. I liked the electronic feedback screen in front of every immigration counter. You could click "satisfactory" if the service was good, or not if it was unsatisfactory. A friendly smile rather than a stern look from immigration officers would certainly make for a more hospitable visit.

Navigating domestic transit in Guangzhou was quite uneventful, except that the walk from the international terminal to the domestic one was rather long. Free buggies or wheelchairs for the less mobile or elderly would have been quite welcome.

COMPLIMENTARY WIRELESS INTERNET

As a modern traveller with gadgets and all manner of technological devices, I am used to complimentary wireless services in well-known airports. As such, the fact that the two airports I visited in China had no such services disappointed me greatly. I did, eventually, find a smartphone charging port and power outlet at the waiting area in Guangzhou, but had to pay for the WiFi services.

South Korea is quite different when it comes to wireless connectivity. When I was at the biggest fish market in Incheon last year, I was pleasantly surprised to find free WiFi services there. No wonder South Korea is ranked No. 1 in the world in terms of high-speed internet penetration.

Security in the air is still tight. During a flight on a Chinese carrier, I wanted to use my mobile phone to make some notes and list down some observations. The flight attendant told me my handphone should not be used at all during the flight, even if it was in airplane mode.

Airplane mode is basically a feature that allows passengers to use a mobile phone safely on a plane in flight by turning off the device's ability to send and receive wireless data signals, which could potentially interfere with the aircraft's communication systems. However, the attendant was adamant and reiterated that no mobile phone could be used in the air, even as an alternative device. This was in contrast to other airlines that I am used to.

Chapter 11
STOWAWAY WOES

I'm going to discuss a rather odd topic that probably will not pertain to you, especially if you're comfortably seated on a plane reading this. But it may interest you: stowing away.

Many readers of my column have asked me this: How is it possible that some stowaways have survived and what kind of impact would their 'flight' would have on the human body?

In June 2015, there was a news report of a stowaway incident on a British Airways Boeing 747. The flight from Johannesburg in South Africa to London covered 6,000 miles and took about 12 hours. One of two stowaways fell from the plane and onto the roof of a house as the plane was approaching Heathrow airport and died. A second man who was hiding in the wheel bay survived the journey, but suffered injuries.

Survival for stowaways seems to be a matter of luck. As to why people resort to such desperate and dangerous measures, I am not qualified to comment. Perhaps, some believe the risks are worth taking, while others are simply ignorant about the dangers involved.

HAZARDS AND DANGERS

What are the dangers then? A stowaway risks being crushed when the landing gears are retracted, or falling from a great height when the doors are opened, thus facing a rapid reduction in oxygen supply to the body. There is also the danger of being exposed to extremely cold temperatures, which leads to frostbite, and incredibly high noise levels, which can cause deafness.

If a stowaway is lucky enough to escape falling off the plane or being crushed by its wheels, the next hurdle is combating altitude-induced oxygen loss in the bloodstream, which leads to unconsciousness.

A stowaway risks being crushed when the landing gears are retracted.

Inside the aircraft, this lack of oxygen is addressed through cabin pressurisation, whereby the internal pressure of the plane is increased. For example, at 25,000 feet, without oxygen, a person's TUC — how long he or she can function with reasonable competence — is about three to six minutes. By the time the plane levels off at 35,000 feet, TUC is reduced to just 30 to 60 seconds. By pressurising the plane, most modern airliners are able to create a comfortable cabin altitude of about 8,000 feet, when the actual altitude is 35,000 feet.

This is necessary because as the plane climbs, the air becomes thinner and the amount of oxygen absorption decreases. Pressurising the cabin as the plane ascends has the effect of squeezing the air back together, recreating the dense, oxygen-rich conditions found closer to the ground. Hence, passengers remain comfortable in a pressurised cabin, whereas a stowaway hiding in the unpressurised wheel bay would gradually become unconscious.

In 2003, a young man mailed himself in a large box that was put on a cargo plane from New York to Dallas, Texas. He lived to tell the tale, but only because the box was loaded into a pressurised cargo hold.

When a plane is flying at 35,000 feet, the outside air temperature is about minus 56 degrees Celsius. Inside the aircraft cabin, the temperature is kept to a comfortable 25 degrees Celsius. A stowaway hiding in the unheated wheel compartment would suffer extreme cold and frostbite.

AGAINST THE ODDS

So, how have some stowaways survived? According to medical experts, some people enter a state of semi-hibernation under certain low-temperature conditions, whereby their metabolism slows down and the need for oxygen is reduced.

One example is the 2001 case of a 13-month-old baby who wandered outside in the bitter cold in Alberta, Canada, clothed only in a diaper. When she was found face down in the snow, her heart had stopped and her toes and mouth were frozen solid. But hours later, she was revived. Doctors agreed that it was slowed metabolism that saved her life.

This may explain how, in April 2014, a teenage stowaway on a Boeing 767 flight from California to Hawaii stayed alive. Then again, perhaps residual heat from some of the hot pipes nearby might have warmed the plane's wheel bay where he was hiding.

Hypothermia can also occur when the body temperature drops, usually after prolonged exposure to extremely cold weather.

It is difficult to pinpoint the minimum amount of oxygen that humans need to survive. People have made it to the top of Mount Everest (29,029 feet) without the use of an oxygen tank. In 1986, a 35-year-old man stowed away in the wheel-well of an aircraft bound for Miami, in the US, from Panama and survived the three-hour flight at 39,000 feet! Ten years later, a 22-year-old stowaway survived a 10-hour British Airways flight from Delhi to London, but suffered severe hypothermia. It is thought that his body went into a frozen state of suspension. The man's younger brother, who had stowed away in the nose wheel compartment, was not so fortunate.

Statistics show that about 75% of stowaways fail to reach their destinations.

It is therefore imperative that security at airports around the world introduce even more stringent measures to thwart stowaways. These measures could annoy some travellers, but the safety of guests, as well as those who may want to attempt the desperate act, is paramount.

Chapter 12

WRONG LANDING STRIP, CAPTAIN!

In the early days, when planes flew low and slow, pilots would follow familiar rivers, roads or railway lines to get to their destination. This is not possible today because airliners are big, fast and noisy, which means they have to fly high and above the clouds.

ACCURATE AIR NAVIGATION

Today, with modern navigational aids such as the Global Positioning System, any destination, anywhere in the world, can be easily located. GPS accuracy is precise. For example, after flying about 5,500 miles from Kuala Lumpur to London, a plane can still locate the exact runway of the destination, just as the GPS in your car can locate the correct road to your friend's home.

Accurate air navigation is possible because the exact routes are programmed into the plane's computers before departure. In theory, the pilot would only need to cross-check his position following the route on the map. However, in practice, owing to aircraft traffic, sometimes there may be interruptions along the route and the pilot may have to make minor corrections.

THE PERFECT VISION MYTH

At times, on arrival at a destination, a pilot may need to look out of the cockpit window. If he is short- or long-sighted, he can still use his glasses. Pilots no longer need to have perfect vision. That was a requirement in the past, for example during World War I, when pilots had to have sharp vision to identify enemy aircraft.

Today, pilots are permitted to wear glasses as they need not look out for the correct airways, like a car driver looking for

Pilots no longer need to have perfect vision.

road signs. Additionally, most modern aircraft can actually land blind during auto-landing with almost zero visibility, provided the airfield is equipped with the appropriate Instrument Landing System (ILS).

USE OF RADAR SERVICES

Another way to locate the correct airport runway is to make use of radar services from air traffic control on the ground. If the weather is good, the pilot will be able to see the runway. While low visibility during foggy weather can be intimidating, ILS can come to the rescue. If the pilot is properly certified, auto-landing in very low visibility is not a problem as long as there are good navigational aids, reliable radar services and well-managed computers on board the plane.

FINDING THE RIGHT RUNWAY

Despite all these great navigational aids, we still read news reports about airline pilots landing on the wrong runways at some airports. How is this possible?

In the US a few years ago, two commercial airliners, a Boeing 737 and Boeing 747, landed at the wrong airport. First, such mistakes should not be made by a well-trained airline captain. As a general rule, aircraft commanders must have a thorough knowledge of the arrival airfield before even setting course for it. If they are unfamiliar with the runway, they should study, among other things, identification of the runway, for example, Runaway 18, its surface condition, length and width, as well as taxiways leading to their parking bay.

Invariably, investigations tend to indicate that wrong landings happen because the pilots confused a parallel runway with their target runway, or mistook a nearby airport for their intended destination because they failed to cross-check their flight instruments. The pilots elected to trust their eyes more instead of their navigational aids.

Such mistakes are now classified as pilot error. The airline industry's response to such embarrassing and other pilot-induced errors is to increase training in crew resource management.

AERODROME CATEGORISATION

To reduce errors among new pilots, most airlines group airfields under categories — A, B and C. Category A aerodromes are generally easy airfields, while those under Category B require some form of briefing. Category C comprises difficult aerodromes that may even require a simulator check or a visit to the airfield before the pilot is allowed to fly into them.

In addition, most airlines require their pilots to operate

following Instrument Flight Rules (IFR) even if the weather is good. By doing so, the safety of the plane is placed under the supervision of air traffic control. The plane would then be guided by radar to the correct runway.

When flying under IFR, the plane is properly set up with the correct runway and ILS on its computer. Also, a proper briefing by ATC is done after checks by both pilots. If they fail to do this, mistakes are more likely to happen.

However, if the pilots declare that they can see the ground or are flying under Visual Meteorological Conditions (VMC), responsibility then shifts to the captain. Herein lies the danger as humans can make mistakes and land on the wrong runway, especially at a similar airfield nearby.

INSTANCES OF PILOT ERROR

On Oct 15, 2012, an Indonesian airline grounded a captain and first officer for landing at the wrong airport. The Boeing 737 they were commanding was operating a service to Minangkabau International Airport in West Sumatra, but the aircraft touched down instead at another airport that had long been closed to commercial flights and was used only by the air force. The two airports are less than 10 miles apart and both have a single runway located parallel and close to the coastline. The approach took place in broad daylight, with good visibility.

On Nov 21, 2013, a Boeing 747 cargo plane landed at the wrong airport in Wichita, the US, instead of its intended destination some 12 miles away.

Many wondered how the pilots could have made such a mistake. According to the former chief pilot of flight operations at Boeing in Wichita, it was not unusual for pilots who are unfamiliar with the airport to be confused as the runways at both airfields are closely aligned and almost parallel to each other.

On Jan 12, 2014, a Southwest Airlines Boeing 737 bound for Branson Airport in Missouri, the US, landed at the wrong airfield, also in good weather.

Complacency may be one of the factors that contributed to pilot error. These incidents led one reader to ask how it is possible for such modern jetliners to lose their way. My answer: There was nothing wrong with the aircraft or its instrumentation. The three Boeing planes had good navigational aids. The errors were caused by humans, who are not infallible.

Chapter 13
GOING AROUND

In movies, when a technical problem or crisis occurs during landing, sometimes the air traffic controller cries out, "Abort! Abort!"

Is this term commonly used in the aviation industry? No! In fact, the correct term is "Go around!" I believe "Abort!" is used in films to enhance the dramatic effect of a landing gone wrong.

Going around is a very safe manoeuvre that is often carried out for safety reasons.

In reality, every pilot understands what go around means. I was introduced to this aviation terminology during my first flying lesson on a de Havilland Canada DHC-1 Chipmunk in 1967.

EARLY TRAINING

My first flying lessons were held at No 1 Flying Training School at RAF Church Fenton, 20 miles east of the city of Leeds in the UK. Back then, I was flying the Chipmunk, a two-seater plane used extensively as a primary training aircraft after World War II. It weighed about the same as my car — 900kg — and had a 145-horsepower piston engine, just like that in my vehicle. Unlike other smaller

The Chipmunk (WG 486) that I was trained in when I first started flying.

training planes with side-by-side seating, the Chipmunk had a single front-and-back seating. One would think that it was inconvenient to have the instructor sit behind the student, but this arrangement made the Chipmunk a very successful training aircraft.

Stories of agitated instructors knocking the helmets of trainees were not uncommon. Well, that was the only way trainers could release their pent-up emotion mid-flight! Fortunately, I had a patient instructor and was spared that occasional ordeal even though I was not a fast learner.

I was taught to go around when the runway ahead was blocked by a disabled plane or if I had "screwed up" a landing profile.

ORIGIN OF THE TERM

"Go around" originated from the traditional air traffic pattern that is almost oval in shape, like a huge racing circuit. Arriving aircraft will join the circuit pattern in an orderly manner. If for any reason a plane was not able to make a successful landing, it would just fly back to the normal height and complete another circuit.

Hence the term, which is still used today even though modern jetliners now climb straight ahead instead of using the traditional circuit.

Aborting and going around even just before landing is a safe manoeuvre.

GOING AROUND ON A JET PLANE

Aborting a landing and going around on a piston plane is different compared with on a modern jetliner, with its powerful engines and higher speed.

On a jet plane, going around can be quite work-intensive. It involves pushing the thrust levers forward, retracting the flaps and raising the nose of the aircraft to a specific angle. Then the navigation computers need to be reprogrammed and the automation reset. The pilot also has to call for the checklist and execute various other tasks.

Some pilots have their own personal checklist on top of the airline's procedures for the go-around. They silently remind themselves of the "5 Ups": Power up, nose up, gear up, flaps up, speak up.

FALSE ILLUSION

In marginal weather and at night, a false illusion can sometimes cause disorientation. Have you ever experienced that? For example, you are sitting in a train at a station and the train next to it starts moving. Suddenly, you have the illusion that your train has moved in the opposite direction.

In the air, this false sensation (somatogravic illusion) may be encountered especially in the absence of a clear horizon and you are flying wholly or partly by visual external reference. It is caused by damage or irritation to the vestibular organs in the inner ear that help the human body achieve balance and stability.

In a jet, the linear acceleration of its powerful jet engines gives a false sensation of a steep climb and the automatic response of the pilot is to correct that by pushing the plane's nose down. This can be disastrous.

On Aug 23, 2000, an Airbus A320 flew into the sea during an intended dark night go-around in Bahrain as the result of a false sensation experienced by the pilot. On May 12, 2010, an Airbus A330 descended rapidly to the ground with a high vertical and forward speed in Tripoli, Libya. The aircraft was destroyed by the impact and consequent fire, and all but one of the 104 on board perished.

To overcome false illusions, pilots are continually being trained to be aware of such pitfalls and to trust their flight instruments.

ENSURING A SAFE LANDING

The standard operating procedures of many airlines include a list of conditions that must be satisfied to carry out a safe landing. If one or more of these conditions are not met, a go-around must be performed. Airlines typically require that a plane be stabilised at 1,000 feet above the runway in poor visibility and at 500 feet in clear weather. The crew must also have extended the landing gears, performed the necessary tasks on the checklist and be fully ready for the landing. Otherwise, the captain must abort the attempt.

Most airlines today ensure their pilots abide by the list of conditions by implementing the Flight Operational Quality Assurance (FOQA) safety programme, designed to improve aviation safety through the proactive use of flight-recorded data.

For instance, if the approach speed for a landing is 150 knots, the pilot should not allow the plane to exceed a speed ranging between 10 and 25 knots above 150 knots by the time the plane reaches 1,000 feet above the runway. If the pilot does so, the information will be captured automatically by the computer and he or she will be called up the next morning by the chief pilot of safety to explain the transgression. This is a very effective tool for eliminating bad or unsafe landings.

THE IMPORTANCE OF GOING AROUND

In 2013, there were three accidents that could have been avoided had the pilots gone around in time. Failure to do so early caused an Asiana Airlines Boeing 777 plane to slam into a seawall, a Boeing 737 to break its nose gear because of a very hard landing, and an Airbus A300-600 cargo plane to plough into a hillside short of the runway.

I hope you now understand that going around is a very safe manoeuvre that is often carried out for safety reasons. Crews are encouraged to abort a landing if they think it could jeopardise safety and no questions would be asked by the management.

In the past, every go-around had to be accounted for and some pilots were reluctant to execute it, even in an unstabilised approach. Others were often influenced by the "Get-home-itis" syndrome — when pilots try to reach their destination at all costs.

Chapter 14
COCKPIT CHALLENGES

I was recently asked to identify the most difficult aspects of handling a plane. I think a more interesting question would be: Which of the three main manoeuvres — taxiing, take-off or landing — is the most challenging?

The truth is, there is no definitive answer. Different pilots find each of these phases of flight challenging in different ways, and this is largely influenced by their personal flying experience, the type of aircraft they are flying, as well as environmental conditions. In fact, an airline or general aviation pilot would justifiably have different views.

A plane taxiing out of the gate for take-off.

From my perspective as a commercial airline pilot, the answer is most certainly the landing aspect of the flight. Let me elaborate on the three phases and the unique challenges posed by each.

TAXIING FOR TAKE-OFF

It is a common perception that a flight begins with take-off and concludes upon landing. This couldn't be further from the truth. The fact is a flight actually begins and ends at the parking bay, from the moment a plane taxis out on its own power and heads towards the runway, until after the aircraft lands and taxies into a parking bay at its intended destination.

A good taxi is smooth and follows the centre line of the taxiway or runway. Big planes such as the Airbus A380 and Boeing 777 have cameras to guide them. Smaller aircraft, however, lack this luxury and pilots have to rely on their expertise to remain centred on the runway and anticipate turns on the ground.

Taxiing in poor visibility is often an uphill task for a pilot. I once landed in Zurich, Switzerland, in bad weather conditions and had to request that a high-visibility "Follow Me" truck guide me to the appropriate parking bay.

When the weather is good though, taxiing a plane is relatively easy. The captain merely turns a tiller (steering wheel) with his left hand at low speed and then switches to

An Airbus A330 making an approach to touchdown with landing gears extended.

using the rudder pedals with his feet to maintain the centre line of the runway during take-off.

UP, UP AND AWAY!

The take-off phase begins when the thrust levers (throttles) are applied and the plane starts moving at a high speed before lifting off the ground. Large jet engines are very powerful and normally, a reduced take-off thrust is used to prolong engine life.

During take-off, the plane accelerates to a lift-off (rotation) speed prior to getting off the ground. The term "rotation" is often used because the aircraft pivots around the axis of its main landing gear while still on the ground. The nose is then raised (rotated) to increase the lift generated by the airflow across the wings.

The speed needed for lift-off is relative to the motion of

the air. For instance, a headwind reduces the ground speed needed for take-off as there is greater flow of air over the wings. A typical take-off air speed for jetliners, depending on their weight, is in the 130-to-155-knots range.

A pilot needs to take note of three important speeds during take-off. The first is the decision speed. It marks the point after which an emergency stop is no longer possible and the plane is committed to continue with the flight. If the pilot, for any reason, decides to abort the take-off, it must happen before the plane reaches this speed.

The second is the rotation speed, whereby the pilot pulls the flight control column towards him for the plane to lift off the runway. It is important for the pilot to precisely determine this speed. If a plane is rotated too early, its tail may scrape the runway (tail strike).

Finally, there is the safety speed at which the plane becomes safely airborne, even in the extremely unlikely event of engine failure. It needs to be emphasised that take-off is a very safe procedure. The captain's training requires that he knows exactly what to do based on the speed that the plane has attained. As a stringent backup measure, engine failure exercises are frequently practised in the flight simulator.

AND WE HAVE TOUCHDOWN...
Generally, landing a plane is trickier than taking off as there

are many variables present in the environment. For instance, if the plane is estimated to land on a wintry day with poor visibility because of fog, a pilot has to plan for an automatic landing.

Autolanding, which is always monitored by the captain, is a very safe procedure as the flight computer guides the plane all the way till touchdown. This system is capable of landing the plane safely even when visibility or cloud ceiling is very low. In fact, without automation, many airports would be closed for landing during winter as foggy conditions are prevalent.

Landing a plane in windy conditions is a challenge for the best of pilots, and is therefore restricted according to the strength of crosswinds, which may cause difficulties. For the Airbus A330, for example, a limit of 40 knots is imposed for landing. Even with this limitation, strong crosswinds necessitate skilful handling by a pilot, who must make use of the rudder to keep to the centre line on the runway.

During touchdown in a crosswind landing, the pilot must remove the drift that the aircraft has been maintaining in order to line up with the runway. Managing this manoeuvre requires expert coordination.

Another situation that tests a pilot's skills is landing in high-altitude airports. A poorly executed approach can result in a hard or heavy landing, which will require the aircraft to be examined thoroughly to determine if repair or maintenance work is required.

In one incident that involved heavy landing in a remote high-altitude airport where the necessary maintenance was not available, the plane had to be flown back to the main airport with its landing gears extended. This was a pricey affair as it not only involved repair costs; flying with gears extended caused the plane to burn more fuel.

AS UNPREDICTABLE AS THE WEATHER

At the end of the day, whether the take-off or landing is trickier greatly depends on the conditions that exist at that given point in time.

A manual landing is certainly more challenging owing to variable environmental conditions. But while no commercial airliner is capable of taking off automatically, the landing can definitely be carried out entirely by automation.

And if the destination airport is equipped with autolanding facilities, the plane's in-built automation makes the touchdown a piece of cake.

Landing is my favourite part of a flight as it means that I've safely flown my passengers to their destination. My daughter, on the other hand, loves take-offs, when the engine hums and builds up to a crescendo before a burst of power lifts the plane into the sky.

Chapter 15
SAFE SNAPS

As smartphones evolve, their built-in cameras become more powerful and the range of photo-editing apps is ever more creative.

Given the ease of whipping out a handphone to capture a moment and share it via social media, it's not surprising that the smartphone, in all its incarnations, is everywhere. Therefore, travellers are often surprised to learn that in certain locations and situations, it may not be acceptable to be snap-happy.

CONFUSING SITUATIONS

A guest recently wrote to me asking whether there are rules that prohibit taking pictures or videos on board a plane. A member of the cabin crew had approached him and requested that he erase the pictures he had just taken with his phone. He could not understand the rationale for that and asked whether this activity might have any bearing on the safety of the plane.

I understand how precious pictures can be, especially those that capture unforgettable moments during one's travels. As far as I know, there are no international laws prohibiting the taking of photos inside the cabin. However, individual carriers have the right to implement and enforce their own rules, as do airport authorities.

Let's take a look at a few examples.

TO DELETE OR NOT TO DELETE?

A musician was recently waiting at an airport terminal for his flight when he decided to take a picture of an aircraft with his phone. A gate agent noticed him doing that and demanded to know why he was snapping pictures of the aircraft and accused him of being a security threat. He politely showed her the pictures and offered to delete them if he had breached any airport security protocol and explained that he had been unaware of any prohibition against taking pictures of planes.

On the ground, most airports and military installations do not allow pictures to be taken within their compounds, citing "security reasons". To me, this does not make much sense in this day and age of the internet, as one can view close-up images of the cockpit, cabin and aircraft of almost every airline in the world on sites such as Airliners.net! It appears that attempts to restrict photography are based on misguided fears about the dangers they may pose.

Often, the decision on whether a guest is permitted to take pictures is made by the airport authorities. Most airlines

do not publish prohibitions against taking photos of their aircraft, while some, like Qantas, openly permit the use of cameras at any time, as outlined in their cabin safety cards. This can be quite confusing for travellers.

As a rule of thumb, always use common sense. In many airports where guests have to walk on the tarmac to move between the main terminal building and an aircraft, airport authorities usually request that photographs not be taken. This is because of safety concerns. As there is traffic on the tarmac, a guest walking around snapping pictures of his family with the aircraft in the background (a great photo op for sure!) may obstruct traffic, or risk stepping onto the path of an airport vehicle. Now, imagine the potential dangers if more than one family decides to orchestrate similar family shots.

PROTECTION AND DISCRETION

Often, the prohibition on photography in aircraft cabins is put in place to protect flight and cabin crew, as well as guests.

I remember an incident where a passenger faced negative reaction when he started filming an incident on board. In this case, a member of the cabin crew had been reluctant to board a family with a sick child as there were concerns about the child's fitness to travel. The family explained that the child was suffering from cancer but had been medically certified as fit to fly. However, as another member of the cabin crew also felt that boarding the child would expose the airline and crew to risks if anything untoward were to happen during the flight, the family was asked to return to the terminal building.

The above occurred a few days after another cancer patient was asked to disembark from a plane under similar circumstances. This prompted the passenger to record his conversation with the crew on his smartphone, as he felt it was wrong for the airline to deny passage to the sick child. When the guest refused to delete the video recording, he was escorted off the flight and rebooked on a subsequent one.

The reason for this? The crew no longer felt safe after being recorded by the passenger. Now, I am not going to debate the decision made by this airline with regards to the passage of the sick child as every airline has its own carriage policies, but I can comment on the outcome.

After this incident was highlighted in the media, the airline admitted that since it did not have a clear policy on photography, its employees did not have the legal right to demand that the guest delete his recording. However, in explaining the unfortunate incident, the airline did make reference to protecting the privacy of other passengers and the safe and secure operations of the aircraft.

As the speed and ease with which we capture and relay information evolves, it is imperative that laws governing such modes of communication offer clearer guidelines that allow for certain freedoms and also protection and privacy. I imagine it can be pretty intrusive to be photographed or recorded in the course of conducting one's everyday duties. Imagine if someone did that to you in the office if he disagreed with the way you handled a particular matter?

As with all matters, discretion is always advised.

So, can an airline actually stop you from taking photos? The answer is yes. While photography cannot be prohibited in public places, the prevention of photography on private property is legitimate. That decision rests with the owner of the property, which would be whichever airline you choose to fly.

ARE CAMERAS SAFE?

A conventional camera is classified as a non-intentional transmitter of radio signals, meaning that it would not interfere with airplane operations. Its usage is not as critical as a smartphone, which intentionally transmits radio signals when used as a communications tool.

Most airlines allow cameras to be used on board to record a personal event, but taking snapshots of the crew or other passengers without permission is a no-no. So, it appears that one can take pictures without annoying other passengers, any time when electronic devices are permitted, which on some airlines means only before the doors are shut or above 10,000 feet. If a member of the cabin crew requests that you put your smartphone away, it's advisable to do so as they usually have the backing of air regulations.

MY ADVICE

The best policy to avoid any controversy concerning grey areas such as taking photos on an aircraft is to comply with regulations. This means stopping when requested and, if necessary, deleting videos and pictures too. By all means, take pictures of the amazing food you have been served on the flight and go crazy with selfies of your airplane static frizzed hairdo. But if you have a niggling feeling that what you are doing infringes on the privacy of another person, or if you would feel uncomfortable being recorded yourself, then it is best to put your smartphone away.

Chapter 16
HAVE A PLEASANT FLIGHT

My first international flight was in 1967 on a British Eagle Britannia, a four-engine propeller plane, from Changi Airport in Singapore to Heathrow, London. It transited through Colombo, Sharjah (in the United Arab Emirates) and Rome. I was 21 then and could not remember if it was a pleasant flight, but it was definitely exciting. I did not know what to expect on such a long-haul flight and accepted everything as

A British Eagle Britannia in 1967

Image by Ken Fielding

part of the adventure. Today, having flown a total of 25,500 flight hours in the cockpit and many flights as a passenger, I believe I have enough experience to comfortably provide some information on how to make your flight as pleasant and enjoyable as possible.

CREATE A CHECKLIST

If you are a frequent traveller, it is advisable that you prepare a checklist for a hassle-free journey. The most important item on that list is your passport; in addition to having it with you, don't forget to check its validity. There was a case where a traveller's important business trip was disrupted because he took his wife's passport by mistake and only realised it at the immigration counter! It is therefore crucial to ensure you have your own travel document and that it has a validity period of at least six months.

Below is a recommended checklist:
- Passport and visa — Ensure that it is yours and check its validity. Also ensure you have the proper documentation to enter whichever country you are heading for.
- Tickets — Keep your tickets in your hand luggage, note the web reference number and do an electronic check-in if possible.

- Hotel – Book your accommodation in advance and note the reference number.
- Travel insurance – Buy it for the duration of your holiday.
- Foreign currency – Exchange your money in various denominations, including coins, for taxis, tips and so on.
- Luggage – Any liquids or gels in your hand luggage will need to be less than 100ml and packed in a clear plastic bag for inspection.
- Magazines, books or e-books.
- Mobile phone, laptop and electronic device chargers, plus an international plug converter.
- Relevant medication, if you have any health issues, plus charcoal tablets just in case.
- Driving licence and identification cards.
- Medical letter or note if you cannot go through a metal detector (for example, if you have a pacemaker).

WHAT YOU CAN CARRY

You will also need to check the hand luggage regulation on your flight, for instance, whether you can carry one more bag in addition to a handbag or laptop bag. The dimensions are also important as some carriers have a size limit on the hand luggage allowed. Check the weight of your check-in luggage as excess weight will mean incurring excess charges. Don't forget to write your name and address on a luggage tag in case your luggage gets lost. Another handy tip is to have something colourful or striking, like a brightly coloured ribbon, attached to your luggage handle as this will make identifying it on the carousel much easier. Also remember not to pack your passport or money in your check-in luggage.

TIMELINESS

Always give yourself sufficient time to proceed through the various checkpoints at the airport. With security becoming more stringent, catching international flights at busy airports can be a long, arduous process. Rushing to the airport or being delayed by traffic jams can create unnecessary stress, so, as a general rule of thumb, always leave for the airport at least three hours before your departure time.

BIN ALL EXCESS LIQUIDS

After the Sept 11, 2001 attacks, any liquid or gel exceeding 100ml is not permitted in the cabin and will be confiscated. Bin them before going through the security checkpoint to save time. Security rules pertaining to laptops have also changed: Now you have to remove your laptop from its bag during the security screening. Some random security checks may require you to switch it on during inspection to ensure that it is in working condition and not being used to stash anything illegal or hazardous.

ON THE PLANE

Ensure that your hand luggage is light enough for you to lift and place in the overhead compartment. Before stowing your bag, it's a good idea to take out any items you may need during the flight, especially if your seat is by the window, as you may disturb other passengers if you are constantly moving in and out of your seat. If you have a small piece of hand luggage, you should be able to fit it under the seat in front of you and still have enough legroom.

ENTERTAINMENT AND COMFORT

To keep yourself occupied, bring along reading materials, portable game consoles or movie players. If you are travelling with young children, bring a portable DVD player or tablet to help keep boredom at bay. Do remember to bring headphones to avoid disturbing other passengers. Always ensure that your electrical devices are fully charged prior to your flight. Wear comfortable clothes on long-haul flights and don't forget to bring a light jacket as the cabin can get a bit chilly at times. Also, moisturisers and eye drops come in handy as the air in the cabin can be dry.

INFLIGHT WIFI

Previously, the usage of certain personal electronic devices was not allowed during flights. However, many carriers now offer inflight internet services for a fee. This allows passengers to stay connected for business or leisure while in the air. Travellers on business trips usually welcome the opportunity to stay productive during their flight. Although the connection may not be as fast as on the ground, the ability to read and send emails from 35,000 feet is a great advantage!

BRING A SLEEP KIT

I always carry my sleep kit with me whenever I fly, even on short trips. This consists of a U-shaped travel pillow and eyeshades to block out the light. Remember not to over inflate the pillow as it will expand when the cabin altitude increases during the climb. Ear plugs will help you sleep better if you want to block out engine noise or if there is an upset baby on board who is suffering from flying discomfort.

EXERCISE TO REDUCE RISK OF DVT

It is not advisable to stay seated for long periods of time, especially on long-haul flights. Inflight magazines usually have a section on light exercises, such as shoulder or knee lifts and foot pumps, which you can safely do on an airplane. It is also good to take a walk around the cabin during the cruising phase of the flight. Moving around the cabin and stretching is said to help prevent deep-vein thrombosis (DVT), a condition that occurs when blood clots form in deep veins, usually in the calf or thigh. DVT can be catastrophic if the clot dislodges and travels to the heart, lungs or brain, forming an embolism. The exact cause of DVT is unknown, but the risk of developing it increases with prolonged immobility and dehydration, as well as with age.

Other factors can aggravate DVT risk, such as hormone therapy, the use of contraceptive pills, pregnancy, smoking, post-surgery recovery, advanced cancer and obesity. To reduce the risk of DVT, avoid consuming caffeinated and alcoholic beverages, drink more water or fresh fruit juices to improve hydration, and wear support stockings, which are designed to improve blood flow in the legs. Some doctors recommend taking aspirin, but the side effect of this is that it thins the blood.

ENJOY THE RIDE

No matter what you do to ensure a comfortable flight, it is good to remember that the less stressed you are, the better you will feel when you arrive at your destination. Yes, you will enjoy the journey as part of a great adventure, just as

I did when I flew my first international flight of over 10,800 kilometres!

PART THREE
FLIGHT CREW

Chapter 17

SALUTING THE CABIN CREW

Comprehensive training, a cool head and a big heart all figure in the make-up of the glamorous jet-setting crew.

Captain Sully was praised in the media for the way he handled the Hudson landing, but the other quiet hero of the day was flight attendant Doreen Welsh, who efficiently evacuated the cabin, instructing passengers to jump over the seats to move forward. She was so focused on guiding the passengers to safety that she failed to notice a large cut on her leg.

Flight attendants are trained to handle many tasks on board the plane.

Flight attendants have been called "trolley dollies", a term coined in an earlier era in reference to how cabin crew served drinks and other refreshments from a trolley. In the early days of aviation, the job of a flight stewardess (the preferred terminology now is flight attendant or cabin crew) was an enviable one as it allowed these sophisticated and fashionable women to fly around the globe and stay at top-notch hotels in exotic places while visiting wonderful attractions beyond the reach of regular folks. People perceived flying to be a dream vocation. However, the job is not without its challenges.

TRIALS AND CHALLENGES

The life of the flight crew in general is one of constant travel, navigating time zones and combating jet lag. A flight attendant's schedule differs with every trip. Some flights are night departures while others take off during the day. Domestic flights rarely involve overnight stays while international flights may mean being away from home for one to four days.

For cabin crew, a typical day begins with them reporting at the flight operations centre, where they check where their airplane is parked, meet other crew members and attend a briefing by the senior cabin crew to discuss any extra services needed for the upcoming flight, such as wheelchair assistance for senior guests or special aid for couples travelling with babies and young children. Being well-prepared ensures a smooth flow during the flight.

Their duties once inside the plane include pre-flight checking of the cabin, and then boarding passengers, assisting them where necessary and making sure that the aircraft compartment is ready for take-off. Once all the passengers have boarded, the crew will do a headcount check and make sure that everyone is buckled up, with their belongings safely stowed. They also perform a safety demonstration to ensure all guests know how to buckle and unbuckle their own seat belts, use oxygen masks if necessary, and are aware of safety protocols aboard in the unlikely event of an emergency.

During the taxi, when the plane moves slowly to the runway for take-off, a senior cabin crew member will make a departure announcement while the rest of the team checks to see that everyone is ready for take-off before notifying the flight crew. At this point, all cabin crew would need to be buckled up safely as well. After the aircraft is airborne but below 10,000 feet, the Sterile Cockpit Rule is observed: Cabin crew are not permitted to communicate with the pilots, except on essential matters that affect safety.

Once the aircraft has climbed above 10,000 feet, or about four minutes after take-off, the fasten seat belt sign is switched off and the cabin crew will begin preparing the food and beverage carts for inflight service. At cruise altitude, a beverage service is provided which may include snacks, or on longer flight, meals too. During the flight, the cabin crew would walk up and down serving drinks and meals, clearing away used cups and eating utensils, attending to passengers' needs, and generally ensuring the comfort of all in their charge.

The flight crew would usually inform cabin crew when they are about 30 minutes from their destination, and issue another reminder when descending below 10,000 feet. This is to give the latter adequate time to prepare for landing and ensure that all passengers have their seat belts securely fastened and baggage stowed away properly.

Upon landing, an arrival announcement is made and once the aircraft is parked at the arrival gate, the cabin crew will commence disembarkation and assist guests where required. Once all the passengers have left the aircraft, the cabin crew perform another check to ascertain that everyone has deplaned and nothing has been left behind. On short-sector flights, the crew perform cabin maintenance during turnaround for the next batch of guests, including scanning the cabin for foreign items, fumigating (to conform to health and agricultural regulations), rearranging aircraft paraphernalia and cleaning the seats — all within 25 minutes on low-cost carriers like AirAsia.

A lot happens in a single day and it can be pretty exhausting as cabin crew are often on their feet the entire time.

RIGOROUS TRAINING

As cabin crew are always in the front line of customer service, they are an important bridge between passengers and the airline. Yet few travellers realise that the exemplary service they are accustomed to comes only second to a flight attendant's top priority — safety.

Flight attendants are trained to be proficient in the use of safety equipment, such as fire extinguishers, first aid kits and defibrillators, and must be able to perform basic medical assistance such as cardiopulmonary resuscitation (CPR). They are also required to memorise the layout and emergency exits on each aircraft type. Before they can be confirmed as cabin crew, candidates have to demonstrate their ability to handle everything, from first aid to life-saving procedures, in a calm and professional manner. To ensure that they are always up to date, cabin crew are required to undergo a refresher course every year.

You may also have noticed cabin crew requesting guests to return their seats to an upright position, open window shades and switch off electronic devices prior to take-off and landing. These are necessary safety protocols that the crew are tasked with enforcing.

Cabin crew are also trained in soft skills to defuse any tense situation on board before it gets out of hand. Failing that, they are trained to restrain unruly guests, but only as a

The cabin crew's job comes with interesting challenges.

last resort and only if they believe that person to be a threat to other passengers on the flight.

TOUGH PREREQUISITES

In the heyday of aviation, circa the 1960s, there were strict requirements for flight attendants. Back then, female cabin crew were not permitted to marry or have children, and were even required to retire by the age of 32. As a result, most women averaged just 18 months on the job. Today, many of these rules have been relaxed. Marriage restrictions have been abolished and the mandatory retirement age is no longer an issue. Some retired flight attendants who have had children have even been re-employed; they are known as "flying mothers".

Rules imposed on recruitment today are generally centred on safety. For instance, for height requirements, cabin crew have to be tall enough to reach the overhead compartments. This is to ensure they are able to help passengers properly stow their baggage overhead.

At AirAsia, the typical requirements advertised for cabin crew are a minimum height of 157cm and a maximum height of 170cm for women, and between 170cm and 180cm for men; fluency in English and the local language; an outgoing, vibrant and fun personality, inexhaustible smiles and energy; good communication skills and a positive attitude. Cabin crew are usually aged between 20 and 35 years, and there are no restrictions on marriage or having children. Here, AirAsia looks for natural team players who are dedicated to providing excellent service and can work with people of all cultures and backgrounds. This is because the airline's dynamic workforce is extremely diverse, with people coming from across the Asean region and beyond, and guests today are from all walks of life.

ACKNOWLEDGING THE UNDERAPPRECIATED
It is the responsibility of the cabin crew to ensure the comfort

and well-being of all passengers on board throughout the journey. To do this, cabin crew undergo rigorous training to comply with the standards set globally by the International Civil Aviation Organization (ICAO).

As such, the term "trolley dollies" is discourteous. It does not adequately describe the skills and responsibilities of the amazing cabin crew who dedicate themselves to the service of passengers. They deserve our utmost respect and I, for one, am honoured to have served alongside outstanding cabin crew who proved time and again that they have both professionalism and heart. In fact, AirAsia made history when it became the first low-cost carrier to be selected as Asia's Leading Cabin Crew at the prestigious 2015 World Travel Awards (Asia and Australasia) and again when it won the World's Best Inflight Service at the 2016 World Travel Awards. These incredible accomplishments just go to show that low-cost does not mean compromising on quality.

Chapter 18
AN AVIATOR'S ASCENT

The flying profession seems to attract people from varied backgrounds, including engineers, dentists, lawyers and even medical professionals. Recently, a doctor surprised me by seeking advice on becoming an airline pilot.

You would expect a medical practitioner, someone who commands respect in his field because of his seniority and special expertise, to move laterally and, perhaps, become an aircraft commander. Unfortunately, it does not work that way. He still has to start at the bottom of the aviation ladder.

FROM PILOT TO CAPTAIN

Promotion to the position of aircraft commander in Asia is generally faster than in the West. This has led many to think that younger Asian captains are less experienced.

It is a myth that 'younger' Asian captains are less experienced.

This is not true. In the West, cadet pilot programmes are uncommon, and the majority of airline pilots start their career in general aviation and build up their flying hours along the way. As such, it is not uncommon to see a 50-year-old first officer in the US with about 15,000 hours under his belt still waiting for an upgrade to commander in a legacy airline.

In Asia, on the other hand, cadet pilot programmes are available and airline-sponsored pilots are well-trained from day one. A pilot with about 4,500 to 5,000 flying hours can become a captain of a jetliner within seven to 10 years from the day he is specially recruited to undergo rigorous training. A pilot may be as young as 26 to 28 years old when he first earns his four bars, the golden or silver stripes on the shoulder that indicate the rank of captain. Rigorous training prepares pilots to assume the role at a younger age without compromising on expertise.

UNIFORM AND RANK

Airline pilots must be seen to be smart-looking to exude confidence. The first pilot uniforms were introduced in the early 1930s by the now-defunct Pan American World Airways, better known as Pan Am. In the beginning, Pan Am operated seaplane services from the US to Britain and France. Hence, pilots' attire resembled naval officer uniforms.

They were designed with the intention of reassuring nervous passengers so that they would feel more confident about their "overseas" journey.

Today, practically every airline in the world has uniforms similar to the naval-style Pan Am designs even though flying boats are no longer used in the industry.

With the advancements in the modern cockpit, fewer humans are needed to operate planes today. As such, the industry has mostly done away with flight engineers, navigators and radio operators on planes with the introduction of computers, the GPS and satellite communication. That leaves only a pilot (captain) and co-pilot (first officer) in the cockpit.

Sometimes, on medium-haul flights of nine to 10 hours, an additional crew known as a cruise pilot comes on board to satisfy flight crew rest rules, which stipulate that a member must not fly for more than a certain number of hours to prevent fatigue.

In some airlines, the cruise pilot is known as a second officer. This pilot operates the plane from the captain's seat outside the critical phases of the flight such as take-off and landing, and from 20,000 feet or higher.

While all pilots wear gold or silver pilot wings that are either made from metal or embroidered on their black or dark blue blazers, one can determine each crew member's duty by the uniform and rank shown. A captain has four stripes either in gold or silver on the epaulettes and four stripes on the sleeves of the blazer. A first officer would sport three stripes and a second officer, two. Depending on the airline, a second officer under training may wear a single stripe on his epaulette.

ROLES AND PROMOTION

Many people have the impression that the co-pilot or first officer is merely an apprentice who assists the captain. In reality, first officers are the second-in-command and are trained in the same skills as the captain. They normally share flying duties equally: The captain flies the outbound leg and the first officer flies the return one, or vice versa. When a captain is incapacitated, owing to a heart attack for instance, the first officer is fully competent to land the plane safely. It is nothing heroic, as often portrayed by the media, because he is trained to do so.

The difference between a captain and a first officer is that the former generally has more flying experience. How then is a first officer evaluated before he is promoted? Many airlines promote their pilots based on seniority within the company. As such, a first officer may sometimes be older in age or have more flying hours than a captain by virtue of having gained experience at other airlines or in the military.

If you see a senior first officer with three stripes, this generally means he has passed most of the requirements for captaincy and will be ready when a command position becomes available. Before being promoted, he will be interviewed and thoroughly checked in a flight simulator, flying in the captain's seat.

Only after it has been confirmed that the first officer is adequately trained will he be allowed to command a flight with commercial passengers.

CREDENTIALS AND ATTRIBUTES

Owing to the limited positions available, only the best candidates are selected to be pilots. Younger readers out there, do you think you have what it takes to be one?

Besides a strong academic background, especially in maths, science and English, you must, among other things, have excellent communication skills and lots of self-confidence, be able to make prudent decisions under pressure, be good at problem-solving and be physically fit.

Of course, having all these attributes does not automatically qualify you to become a member of this exacting flying club. There's more to it. In reality, there are many challenges along the way, but the initial requirement of excellent academic grades is still crucial. To all aspiring pilots, I wish you all the best in achieving your dreams!

Chapter 19
ALLY IN THE SKIES

A first officer or co-pilot is not merely an apprentice who assists the captain.

In terms of rank, the co-pilot or first officer is the more junior of the two pilots in the cockpit and wears two or three stripes on the epaulette.

The normal procedure at the start of a flight is for the captain and first officer to decide between themselves who will be the pilot flying (PF) and the pilot non flying (PNF), now known as the pilot monitoring (PM). For instance, on a return flight from Kuala Lumpur to Bangkok, which then proceeds to Singapore, the captain would normally fly the first leg of the journey from Kuala Lumpur to Bangkok, with the first officer taking over the flight controls for the return journey to Kuala Lumpur. This interchanging flying duty is then repeated on the trip from Kuala Lumpur to Singapore and back.

However, during the time when the co-pilot is the PF, should a situation arise where it is deemed safer for the captain to resume control of the flight, they would switch roles.

Both the PF and PNF positions entail specific duties.

While the PF focuses on the actual flight manoeuvres, the PNF of that particular sector, regardless of whether he is the captain or first officer, will handle radio communications, read the checklists and conduct the pre-flight or external checks, among other things. And together, the captain and first officer will also monitor each other's performance as a team.

For safety reasons, there are certain flight restrictions in place when the co-pilot is flying the plane. On the Airbus A330, for instance, the co-pilot is only permitted to land the plane in crosswinds if the wind strength is not more than 20 knots. The captain, on the other hand, may land the plane so long as the strength of the crosswinds does not exceed 40 knots. Similarly, for a visual landing, the permitted visibility imposed upon a co-pilot is more rigid than the range allowed for a captain, for the simple reason that the latter is more experienced.

MOVING UP THE RANKS

The transition from first officer to captain means that the co-pilot goes from the top of his rank to the bottom of another that is more accountable. With some airlines, experience and skill are not the main criteria for promotion as seniority takes precedence above all else. As such, first officers can become captains only when slots become available, and after fulfilling the seniority requirement.

However, in a growing airline, there are far better opportunities for the second-in-command to graduate to the commander's seat, on the left side of the cockpit.

Today, co-pilots are trained to be assertive and direct when dealing with matters of safety. On the opposite end of the spectrum, there are times when a confident co-pilot may lack the necessary tact in handling difficulties that may arise mid-air.

A case in point was an incident in which, during a descent in total darkness, a co-pilot, rightly assessing that the plane was not stabilised, grabbed the flight controls from the captain and resolved the issue safely. This is a good example of an assertive co-pilot, although the fact remains that he could have handled the situation more diplomatically.

Today, co-pilot training is focused on enhancing flight safety in flight. First officers are trained to be assertive when conveying critical messages. The strategy is for them to first alert the captain of any impending danger, then offer a solution. If no corrective action is taken by the captain, the co-pilot can resort to an emergency assertive procedure, which would normally be initiated when the plane is less than 1,000 feet above ground level.

For example, if a co-pilot determines that a landing should be aborted owing to unsafe conditions, he must communicate this clearly to the captain. If the latter ignores the warning and fails to take the necessary remedial action, the co-pilot's next address would be, "Captain, you must listen, go around now!" If this also fails, he must seize the controls and state, "I have control, going around now!"

This special procedure is imperative in the aviation industry as, in an emergency, there is no time to argue over critical decisions. Any disagreement between the captain and the first officer will be resolved later on. Assertive action by the co-pilot in an emergency is sanctioned by airline management.

WELL-DESERVED RECOGNITION

Regardless of the number of stripes on a pilot's shoulder, both captain and co-pilot perform similar duties, with the exception that the former has more experience and seniority, as well as ultimate authority over the plane.

Both pilots are extensively trained not only on how to fly and land an aircraft, but also how to circumnavigate social awkwardness caused by cultural norms.

In the past, speaking up in the presence of someone more senior may have influenced a co-pilot's actions. But today, heightened awareness and progressive training have enhanced communication between the cockpit crew, resulting in improved teamwork and increased safety in the skies.

I hope travellers will now have new-found respect for the

AirAsia's First Officer Jessica Lee with the Airbus A320.

co-pilot, the ally in the skies who tends to stay in the shadow of the captain. Flying is a team effort and good teamwork under the astute leadership of an experienced captain ensures that each flight is smooth and safe. At the end of the day, that is what every passenger really wants.

Chapter 20
A PILOT'S LIFE

"Wow, you're a pilot? That's fascinating!" I get this remark quite often. The life of an airline pilot conjures up images of travels to exotic destinations, where there are beautiful places to be explored, exciting people to meet and rip-roaring adventures to be had. And these fantasies are exactly why many aspiring pilots chase this dream, which, when viewed this way, can lead to disappointment.

Let me give you some insight into the profession. An airline pilot's primary responsibility is to ensure that he flies the plane and its passengers safely from the departure airport to the destination. This is foremost on our minds, before all those dreams of glamour and adventure. Navigating the skies, seeing the world from above and realising what an awesome responsibility we bear in the safe carriage of our precious cargo — our guests — drive us to be at our best.

EDUCATION AND REQUIREMENTS
So, now that you know what our priorities really are, let us look at how one becomes a pilot. In Malaysia, the minimum

requirement to apply for training is an SPM (Sijil Pelajaran Malaysia) or a GCSE certification with at least five credits, in subjects such as maths, science and English. However, most airlines prefer applicants with an undergraduate degree. Candidates should also be physically and mentally fit, possess good eyesight, should not be colour blind and have a minimum height of 163cm. But these are really just the most basic requirements that will help one get through the door to be accepted for training.

LICENCE AND TRAINING

The first step is to obtain a commercial pilot licence or CPL at a flying training school. This is where most aspiring pilots spend at least 18 months learning the principles of flying, from navigation and aerodynamics to aircraft systems, radio communication and meteorology. During this time, trainees also learn to fly a small plane powered by a propeller engine. To obtain their licence, they have to pass a check flight and oral exams conducted by an examiner from the Department of Civil Aviation. During the flight exam, the candidate will have to execute a number of difficult manoeuvres and handle some emergency exercises designed as a test of proficiency. If the examiner is satisfied with the candidate's performance, a CPL will be issued.

With this, one can apply for more comprehensive and

specific training as a commercial airline pilot. Generally, pilots need to log up to 1,500 flying hours to convert their CPL into an Airline Transport Pilot Licence (ATPL).

At AirAsia, pilot aspirants must obtain an Airbus A320 type rating as the airline operates an A320 fleet, while candidates who wish to fly the long-haul sister airline AirAsia X require an Airbus A330 type rating. Training is done in a flight simulator, where, during check rides, trainees are confronted with various challenging scenarios to test their knowledge, competency, speed in reacting and ability to remain calm under pressure.

SECOND OFFICER PROGRESSION

A pilot graduate from a flying school starts off initially as a second officer in an airline. He has to undergo further training in a flight simulator and is certified proficient on the more-advanced jet plane, such as an Airbus A320, if found competent. This qualification will be endorsed on his flying licence. Only then will he be allowed to undergo line operational training as a second officer with an instructor and a safety co-pilot.

Here again, the trainee will need to prove competency at operating safely without the supervision of a safety co-pilot. If he is found competent and is certified by an instructor, he will continue training for a prescribed number of hours before a final check flight. Only when trainee pilots have passed this last hurdle can they join the airline as first officers. A first officer may serve about seven or eight years and accumulate between 4,500 and 5,000 flying hours before he can be considered for promotion to captain.

LIFE AT WORK

In 2016, career site CareerCast.com rated a commercial pilot's job as the fourth-most stressful job in the world, after firefighter, enlisted military personnel and military general. Flying a plane is a unique skill that requires substantial training before you can do it as professionally, and with good reason, as commercial pilots are responsible for the safety of hundreds of passengers per flight.

Pilots are subject to physical, physiological and psychological stresses that are normally attributed to cockpit noise and fatigue. Other causes of stress are irregular working hours, jet lag and inclement weather conditions.

Would-be pilot candidates need to pass an instrument rating test to assess their ability to fly a multi-engine plane in low visibility. Candidates must be certified by an authorised aviation medical examiner before they can obtain a first-class medical certificate.

Before, you could not become a pilot if your vision needed correction. But many professional pilots now wear

Miss Thailand/Universe 2005 Chanaporn Rosjan turned airline pilot.

glasses or contact lenses, which is allowed as long as their vision is correctable to 20/20.

FUTURE DEMAND

Aircraft manufacturer Boeing recently projected that the world would require some 558,000 new commercial pilots by 2034, with Asia Pacific alone needing 226,000 pilots. But those who wish to pursue this career path should know that there is no guarantee an airline will hire you upon graduation. This is largely because the recruitment of new pilots is slow in some countries, where supply exceeds demand. However, there are signs that the employment rate is gradually improving.

Although the job can be challenging and stressful at times, most pilots wouldn't be happy doing anything else as most of us have dreamed of this career from a very young age. A deep passion for flying is what truly makes a good and dedicated pilot.

# PART FOUR

HEALTH AND MEDICAL ISSUES

Chapter 21
THE DRY DILEMMA

A guest asked me for tips on overcoming the problems caused by dry air. Could the air in the cabin be the reason his nose often bled while flying?

Air inside an airplane can indeed be very dry — it has a very low relative humidity of about 10%. Compare this with the Earth's desert regions, where humidity is around 20% to 25%, or the tropics, where the average relative humidity is 85%.

In the dry environment of the cabin, the skin can lose as much as eight ounces of moisture per hour. According to some medical sources, those with very sensitive skin may find that the delicate sinus membrane inside their nose tends to dry out fairly quickly. This may cause the nose to bleed.

Dehydration may also be the cause of cracked lips, as well as a burning sensation in the eyes, headaches and lethargy. Less obvious consequences of dehydration include stress on the body, reduced mucus production and a weaker immune system.

An adult should drink about eight ounces of water for every hour he is in the air on a long flight.

TACKLING NOSEBLEEDS

To keep hydrated, drink lots of water while on board a plane. The Aerospace Medical Association suggests that an adult drinks about eight ounces of water for every hour he is in the air on long flights. Beverages such as alcohol and coffee should be avoided as they act as diuretics, further dehydrating the body. While flying, one should eat foods that are low in salt and sugar to help the body retain moisture. Finally, be sure to carry a small tube of moisturising lotion to avoid the irritation of dry, flaky skin.

If nosebleeds still occur inflight despite taking all reasonable precautions, it may be necessary to request the assistance of the cabin crew or arrange to see a doctor upon landing.

There are conflicting views among the scientific community as to the main cause of nosebleeds in flight. One doctor commented that if dry air and low humidity were indeed the case, then all those who live in very cold regions of the world and where humidity is very low would experience frequent nosebleeds, as would the majority of air passengers and cabin crew.

Others state that nosebleeds are the result of a common cold or upper respiratory tract infection. In fact, because the nasal blood vessels are very fragile, any irritation to the delicate sinus tissue may cause bleeding.

It has also been shown that there is barely any difference in the incidence of nosebleeds between people working long hours in the cold storage rooms of food processing factories, those working in air-conditioned rooms with low humidity and others working in normal environments.

THE TRUTH ABOUT CABIN AIR

Cabin air may be dry but rest assured that it is very clean. On all modern aircraft, passengers and crew breathe a mixture of fresh and recirculated air. Using this combination rather than fresh air makes it easier to control cabin temperature and maintain a certain level of humidity.

Occasionally, on some flights, you may notice a strong odour similar to that of exhaust fumes in the cabin shortly after pushback. Usually, this only happens when the exhaust air is drawn into the air-conditioning system when the plane engine is started. Wind is often to be blamed because it causes the air to flow back through the air-conditioning system. The smell normally lasts a minute or so, until the engines are running and have stabilised. It may be unpleasant but it is not much different from the fumes you sometimes inhale in your car while stuck in a traffic jam.

Studies have shown that a crowded airplane is no more germ-laden than other enclosed spaces. In fact, an aircraft's underfloor filters have been described by manufacturers as being of hospital quality.

STRANGE EFFECTS

According to Dr Tom Finger, a professor at the University of Colorado's School of Medicine, dry air can affect how we perceive aromas. "Dry air doesn't help our sense of smell either. Typically, odorants are transported to olfactory receptors in the nose via the mucus lining. When the nasal cavity is dried out, the efficiency at which odorants are detected by the brain is reduced. When you lose the olfactory component, you lose much of the flavour component of food," he said.

Low humidity and the dried-out sinus cavity may explain why food sometimes tastes different in the sky, compared with on the ground. You may find that the favourite snack you snuck onto the plane no longer tastes the same.

Taking into account how aroma affects taste buds, airlines usually enhance the flavour of inflight dishes to ensure guests always enjoy their meals in the air. Of course, once you have touched down at your destination, you can always get your local fix.

Chapter 22
EASY, NOT QUEASY

An air traveller shared that his 12-year-old son, who used to be comfortable flying long-haul, had begun to experience motion or air sickness. The vomiting would begin before they left home, and continue throughout the flight.

Although his son enjoyed travelling, the constant vomiting was not only annoying but unpleasant too. He wanted to know the cause and how to treat it so that their travels would be more pleasant.

CONFLICT OF THE SENSES

Motion sickness is caused by a conflict between what is being sensed by the eyes and the ears. The inner ear detects the motion of the plane but the eyes, which are able to focus within the cabin, do not. When the brain receives these conflicting signals, the person develops some aspect of motion sickness.

About one in three people is prone to motion sickness, which can happen when you are on a boat or in a car. There is no difference between motion sickness as experienced at sea, in the air or on a roller coaster.

Vomiting is a symptom of motion sickness, although some people experience nausea — that queasy feeling — first before throwing up.

A PSYCHOLOGICAL RESPONSE

Vomiting is the way the body reacts to something abnormal going on internally. Medically, it is the psychological defence against poisons (neurotoxins). The organ in the body responsible for inducing vomiting is the brain.

Why does the body need protecting? When you are in a plane or on a ship that has no windows, you have no visual reference to what is outside. Inflight, the inner ear tells the brain that it senses motion. However, the eyes relay the message that everything is still and not moving. Because of this conflict of the senses, the brain comes to the conclusion that one of the senses is hallucinating, probably a result of poison ingestion. The brain's immediate response is to induce vomiting to expel the poison.

HELP YOUR CHILDREN

Some children are more prone to motion sickness than others. The aforementioned boy's non-stop vomiting could be more psychological in nature: He might be thinking about previous episodes, which could trigger anxiety. A doctor, especially one who specialises in diseases of the ear or nervous system, would be better qualified to provide an accurate diagnosis.

In any case, one way to reduce motion sickness is to encourage your child to focus on a distant point outside the plane. Avoid activities such as reading or playing hand-held video games, where the eyes stay focused inside the cabin during the journey.

A child on the verge of nausea may feel better when he is able to get some fresh air. Until then, he should avoid strong-smelling, greasy and hard-to-digest foods or snacks. Get the child to fight queasiness by munching some dry crackers.

MY STRUGGLE WITH MOTION SICKNESS

I initially experienced motion sickness during my early flying lessons at the training school at RAF Church Fenton in the UK. Each time I was airborne in the Chipmunk in rough weather, the manoeuvres made me feel sick. My motion sickness caused me great embarrassment as it hampered my flight training.

As a student, I did not carry any sick bag and the only 'containers' available were my leather flying gloves. Happily, in the end, I got over this problem and graduated. But one of my flying colleagues who could not overcome his motion sickness was sent home, dashing his dream of becoming a pilot.

My experience with motion sickness started during my early flying lessons on the Chipmunk.

Fresh air can relieve motion sickness, while odours can exacerbate it. My second experience of motion sickness was actually triggered by a foul odour on the ground. This happened when I hitched a ride in the back of a crammed sports car. I wanted to get out of the flight training school and spend a weekend in London.

I quickly regretted the free ride as it made me feel very sick. I could not stand the smell of the leather seats. The front passenger seat was occupied by my colleague's girlfriend and I was too embarrassed to tell them of my most uncomfortable situation.

I do not know how I managed to hold it in, but I emptied the contents of my stomach as soon as we arrived in London. So, odours may sometimes trigger motion sickness when one is in an enclosed space.

OVERCOMING NAUSEA

The symptoms of motion sickness normally stop when the motion that causes it ceases. However, this is not always true. There are travellers who continue to experience them for a few days after their journey.

Aboard a plane, sit by the window and gaze towards the horizon in the direction of travel. This helps to reorient the inner sense of balance, aligning motion with vision. Choose a seat over the wings, where motion is minimised.

Another way to relieve mild motion sickness is to chew on something. Chewing seems to reduce the adverse effects of the conflict between vision and balance.

Medical researchers have not confirmed the effectiveness of certain remedies such as ginger, camphor or Tiger Balm, although anecdotes suggest they may help.

Some modern medications can help prevent motion sickness and they are best taken before the symptoms surface. Do consult your family doctor for the specific medications.

One can get used to motion sickness over time, like I did, especially if one understands its triggers. Even great astronauts like Frank Borman, the commander of Apollo 8 — the first manned mission to fly around the moon, in December 1968 — was affected by dizziness and nausea.

Chapter 23
FIGHT THE FATIGUE

How do pilots rest sufficiently to fly long journeys? Are they allowed to sleep on long-haul flights? Can sleep deprivation and jet lag jeopardise flight safety? These are questions often asked by concerned travellers.

WHAT IS FATIGUE?

It is a fact that prolonged sleep deprivation and jet lag lead to fatigue. Very simply, fatigue is a state of weariness that could impact a pilot's ability to carry out tasks efficiently. It is therefore understandable that passengers are concerned as the lives of hundreds of passengers on board a plane are in the pilot's hands. Despite rules being implemented by the industry to address this issue, fatigue is an expected condition of modern life.

So what procedures are there to mitigate pilot fatigue?

REST AND RELAXATION REGULATED

In general, pilots are prohibited from flying more than 900 hours a year, or 100 hours in 28 days. They may not be scheduled to fly for more than 30 hours in any seven consecutive days and must be given two days off for every seven days of flying. Since they fly at odd hours, a day off is clearly defined — strictly a 34-hour period with two nights at home.

Pilots' flying schedules depend on whether they have been acclimatised. To be acclimatised, they must have rested sufficiently for three nights in a new destination that is more than two time zones away from the departing airport.

If the pilots have not been acclimatised and begin work very early in the morning, they will be restricted to shorter working hours. All these rules show the aviation industry is fully aware that good rest is very important. They also ensure that pilots are not overworked and, therefore, do not jeopardise the safety of passengers in the air.

Despite the restrictions on flying hours and the emphasis on sufficient rest before flight, there have been infringements.

On Feb 12, 2009, a Bombardier Dash 8 plane belonging to the now-defunct Colgan Air in the US stalled and crashed while landing at Buffalo Niagara International Airport, New York, the result of pilot error. The National Transportation Safety Board (NTSB) found that "the pilots' performance was likely impaired because of fatigue".

FATAL SLEEP
A Federal Aviation Administration (FAA) scientist testified

during the enquiry on the Colgan Air crash that sleepy pilots are likely to make errors in judgement and have trouble concentrating and following multiple sources of information. In this incident, the flight crew lost track of their airspeed and when a warning system was activated, the captain reacted wrongly, pulling the nose of the plane up instead of pushing it down, causing the plane to stall.

On the ground, we have heard of drivers suddenly waking up and realising they had dozed off for a few seconds. Imagine if it were to happen on a flight at a crucial moment!

This actually happened on one of my flights when a trainee pilot fell into sudden slumber on a descent to land. Fortunately, the plane was still very high on the approach. On being awakened, the trainee confessed he was not aware he had dozed off. He admitted that he was extremely tired that day because of improper rest prior to the flight.

NTSB, in a study of crashes of major US carriers between 1978 and 1990 involving flight crew, expressed concern about the effects of fatigue. It stated that half the captains involved had been awake for more than 12 hours prior to the accidents, while half the first officers had been awake for over 11 hours.

On Aug 18, 1993, a Douglas DC-8 collided with the terrain on landing in Guantánamo Bay, Cuba, when the captain lost control of the plane. Investigators found that the flight crew had experienced a disruption of circadian rhythms and sleep loss. They had been on duty for about 18 hours and had flown for almost nine hours.

So, how does a pilot stay awake during the 13 hours to London from Kuala Lumpur. For such long-haul flights, regulations state that the aircraft must be crewed by at least two captains and two first officers, who share the flying duties equally. Hence, each team would fly for six-and-a-half hours only and safety would not be compromised in any way.

TOO TIRED TO FLY

On May 5, 2012 at Munich Airport, an Air Berlin Boeing 747 requested priority landing after its pilots declared a distress call, stating that they were extremely fatigued. The jumbo jet was carrying 335 holidaymakers home from Spain and had to be landed on autopilot. The plane touched down safely.

When the pilot makes a "Pan-Pan" call three times, it indicates the flight is in a state of urgency. When a distress is declared, the plane will be assured of an immediate landing even if it is behind in the queue.

A pilot will only send such a message when he knows he cannot guarantee the safety of the flight. In the Munich incident, it appeared that the crew had been on duty for 10 hours at the time of the distress call and considered their state of alertness to be at the very limit of what was necessary to ensure a safe landing.

This was the first time pilot fatigue had been blamed for such an incident.

RESTED AND READY

If the thought of your pilot lacking the alertness to fly safely worries you, rest assured that safeguards are in place.

Mandatory days off, rest days and acclimatisation, among other precautions, are clearly defined. Problems caused by jet lag are recognised and handled accordingly so that the majority of airline pilots are well rested before take-off.

Your captain and his crew are almost always bright-eyed and bushy-tailed before their flight, regardless of the time.

Chapter 24
SLEEPING ON THE JOB

An interesting report about two pilots leaving the controls to two flight attendants while having a short nap in business class made the news in April 2013.

This happened on an Air India Airbus A320 flight carrying 166 passengers from Bangkok to Delhi. It seems that while the pilots were having their 40-minute break, one of the flight attendants accidentally turned off the autopilot, prompting the pilots to rush back to the cockpit.

Before you start worrying, I must stress that this is absolutely not normal practice. While it is perfectly safe to engage autopilot while cruising, flight attendants are not trained to handle any emergency that may arise. It is, however, standard protocol for at least one flight attendant to be in the cockpit when one of the pilots is on a short break. He or she is there not to take over the pilot's job but to immediately alert the other pilot should the one in the cockpit not be able to operate the plane for any reason.

PILOTS AND POWER NAPS

Can one of the two pilots take a short nap during a flight? The FAA does not explicitly prohibit inflight napping on long-haul flights, but it doesn't permit it either.

According to a NASA study on fatigue, tired people can experience brief periods of "micro sleep" — lapses that last seconds or even minutes during which the eyes are open but the brain is on hold. This is not what you want when your tired pilot is flying a demanding approach through turbulence, rain and low clouds at the end of an eight-hour flight.

On the road, some people may experience a strong urge to nod off during a long, boring drive home. Many motor accidents have occurred as a result of tired and sleepy drivers. Fatigue is a killer. Similarly, there have been a few crashes in which tired pilots made crucial mistakes they might have avoided had they been properly rested. As such, short power naps can sometimes help ensure that pilots and drivers are alert at all times.

The FAA and NASA have tested cockpit napping and found that naps of up to 40 minutes are both safe and effective for pilots on trips of more than seven hours. However, the FAA decided not to pursue this idea vigorously because of the potential lawsuits that could arise should an accident occur while a pilot is napping!

CONTROLLED REST

Despite what certain authorities think, some airlines do permit controlled rests or brief naps on long flights with two pilots, but there is a strict set of conditions. One restriction is that such naps can be taken only during non-critical stages of the flight — that is, the lean period of the cruise — and not during any planned change of flight levels, while performing a fuel transfer, or when there is a forecast of bad weather.

Additionally, the autopilot must be switched on, flight attendants must be informed of the pilot's intention and the other pilot must be fully awake and remain in his seat at all times. A flight attendant must check in over the intercom with the non-sleeping pilot every 15 minutes or so to ensure that everything is normal.

Once the safety procedures have been addressed, the pilot can take a nap of 20 to 40 minutes in his seat in the cockpit. Note that some major airlines which permit such practices stipulate that it only applies to long-haul flights of up to eight hours, with a two-pilot crew.

COCKPIT IN SNOOZE MODE

On Feb 13, 2007, the pilots on board Go! airlines overshot Hilo International Airport in Hawaii. They admitted that they had fallen asleep in the cockpit while the plane was on autopilot. For about 18 minutes, air traffic controllers and other planes attempted to contact the flight crew but were unsuccessful. No one was able to communicate with the aircraft by radio. Both pilots lost their jobs after an investigation by the airline.

FLIGHT ATTENDANTS TO THE RESCUE?

The practice of having a flight attendant inside the cockpit to relieve a pilot who is answering the call of nature gives rise to another question: Is the flight attendant capable of flying the plane in the event that the pilot in the cockpit is incapacitated and the other one is stuck in the toilet?

Flight attendants are generally not capable of flying a plane unless they have privately trained and are licensed to do so. Depending on the airline, flight attendants are not normally allowed to sit in the pilot's seat or manipulate any controls in the cockpit.

The flight attendant sits in the reserve or jump seat to assist in other matters such as retrieving a manual, reading the checklist, or being a communication medium during an emergency when the other pilot is unavailable.

In *Airport 1975*, a flight attendant is able to safely fly a plane with autopilot on until a replacement pilot comes to the rescue. In the movie, a Boeing 747 en route to Los Angeles International Airport from Washington Dulles International Airport collides with a Beechcraft plane during the approach to land. Both aircraft are diverted to Salt Lake City International Airport because of bad weather in Los Angeles.

During the approach, the Beechcraft pilot suffers a massive heart attack and the plane descends onto the approach of the Boeing. The captain is struck in the face by debris and blinded while the first officer is sucked out of the plane during the inflight collision. However, the plane is still flyable. The flight attendant rushes to the flight deck where the captain is able to engage the autopilot before losing consciousness. Subsequently, the flight attendant is able to manoeuvre the plane away from the mountain while a heroic attempt is made to transfer a relief pilot from a helicopter.

In the 1980s comedy *Airplane!*, passengers come down

with food poisoning from eating fish. The cockpit crew, including the pilot and co-pilot, are also affected, leaving no one to fly the plane except the flight attendant. She contacts the control tower for help and is instructed by the tower supervisor to activate the plane's autopilot to get them to Chicago. That is all she can do as she cannot land the plane.

In the tragic Helios Airways Flight 522 incident in 2005, which claimed the lives of all 121 people on board, both the pilots of the Boeing 737 became incapacitated owing to subtle depressurisation that resulted in loss of oxygen. The plane flew on autopilot for more than three hours until it ran out of fuel and crashed.

Apparently, there was a flight attendant on board who had a private flying licence and some flying experience. However, the left engine flamed out as a result of fuel exhaustion just as he made it to the cockpit. It has been speculated that had he reached the cockpit in time, he might have been able to bring the plane down safely, with some assistance from the ground.

AWAKE, ALERT, ALIVE!

In case you're perturbed by the thought of sleeping pilots, rest assured that AirAsia does not practise a sanctioned controlled rest policy or allow its pilots to sleep while on duty. However, we require all our pilots to be fully rested before operating any flight to ensure they are in top form.

Chapter 25
FIT TO FLY

INFECTIOUS TRAVEL

Nobody likes having travel plans disrupted, especially after months of planning. However, when the unexpected happens, one is thrown into a dilemma. What if your child suddenly gets chickenpox?

Unfortunately, you may have to reschedule your family holiday. Can you travel if your child has a minor case of an infectious disease or skin condition? You may, if you have a medical certificate or doctor's letter confirming that she is fit to fly. However, many people are unclear about the general requirements or restrictions.

First, the medical certificate for your child needs to be dated not more than seven days from the date of travel and the parent or guardian is required to sign a limited liability statement upon check-in confirming the child's fitness to travel.

Nevertheless, airlines reserve the right to decline guests suffering from infectious, contagious or chronic diseases that may deteriorate during the journey. They can refuse to board any passenger they believe to be unfit to travel. If there are concerns or indications that a guest may have an infectious disease or skin problem, the airline may require medical clearance.

The main rationale is that airlines have to exercise their responsibility to ensure the safety and well-being of all passengers. This is in compliance with global health regulations and standards.

Below are some illnesses and when it is safe for one to travel.

Chickenpox	Five days after the rashes first appear, provided the spots are scabbed over
Measles	Five days after the rashes first appear
Mumps	Five days after the swelling first starts
Rubella	Five days after the rashes first appear
Tuberculosis	If a medical certificate proves that the guest is not infectious
Whooping cough	Five days after starting antibiotic treatment or three weeks after the onset of symptoms if not treated

CABIN AIR

Some guests wonder how one can still be well after having spent hours with hundreds of other passengers in the cabin, especially when some of them could be ill (or infectious) with medical problems that are not immediately obvious.

Studies have shown that in terms of the spread of contagious diseases, cabin air is often cleaner and healthier than commonly believed.

This is because most modern planes have very good ventilation systems. On most aircraft, air is also circulated through hospital-grade high-efficiency particulate-arresting (HEPA) filters that remove 99.97% of bacteria on board. On average, cabin air is completely refreshed 20 times per hour, compared with just 12 times per hour in an office building.

Misconceptions that cabin air is filthy and germ-laden probably stem from older planes with poor ventilation.

Let me elaborate on the composition of the air on board. The cabin air in today's planes is a mixture of fresh air (from outside the aircraft) and recirculated air (basically the bleed air of the engines). This mixing of cool and hot air helps control the humidity and temperature inside the cabin, keeping passengers comfortable.

Even in very crowded planes, the cabin air is no more germ-laden than that in most other enclosed spaces as the air filters used are of hospital quality.

The other general complaint about cabin air is its dryness. Humidity in the cabin is about 10% mainly because at high altitudes, the moisture content is very low. But the good news is that dryness, though irritating, actually keeps the air clean.

DEAD MAN FLYING

Another inflight issue is what happens when a passenger passes away on a flight owing to a medical condition? This is not a topic that's often raised, but it does happen, and transporting the remains of the deceased is not uncommon.

It happened on one of my flights when I brought my wife along for a stopover in a foreign country. The passenger concerned was afflicted with terminal cancer and his last wish was to be buried in his homeland, Turkey. He was accompanied by a nurse and was not expected to survive the flight, but the crew were not informed about it until his demise.

There is a set of procedures to follow in the event of a death on board. Basically, the deceased passenger must be moved to an empty seat, if available, or brought to a crew rest area to be laid down and covered. If there is no space available, the deceased may be strapped in more tightly, with efforts made to cover the body and place it out of view of other passengers.

On that day, the procedures were carried out so discreetly that the other passengers were not even aware of what had transpired. In fact, my wife told me she was unperturbed by the incident as it was very professionally handled. Additionally, an airline may also be faced with the issue of transporting a dead body back to its home country.

Most countries have a list of requirements pertaining

to that. They include a death certificate issued by the relevant authorities where the death occurred; international transit permits for human remains issued by a local health authority; sanitary-epidemiologic confirmation that the deceased did not die of an infectious disease or in an area with an infectious disease; an embalming certificate and a burial permit, that must all be validated by the consulate in the country of shipping origin.

The airline must also have the necessary equipment to transport the mortal remains in a respectful manner, and also ensure the body does not contaminate perishables and other goods that are being transported by the aircraft. In the event that the next of kin or the airline is not able to fulfil these requirements, the remains of the deceased will not be allowed to be flown out.

SAD FLIGHT HOME

Sadly, I had to fly home a passenger who suffered a heart attack during her holiday in Shanghai. Getting the necessary documentation to leave the country was a greater hassle for the family than transporting the deceased back in the Boeing 777 cargo hold. Coincidentally, I was the captain of this particular flight on that day and the deceased was the mother of a very close friend of mine who was on board. He was extremely grateful that I was ferrying his mother to rest in her place of birth rather than be buried in a distant land. He felt great relief despite his sadness, but I was merely doing my duty to fly the plane home safely for everyone.

SAFE FOR ALL

Illness and death are certainly a part of life, but they become somewhat complicated issues when air travel is involved. The inconvenience of rescheduling a flight owing to the illness of a young child or loved one needs to be weighed against safety guidelines and policies that are set in place to protect every passenger.

Chapter 26
RED, GREEN OR WHITE

COLOUR BLINDNESS

As a general rule, airlines do not employ pilot aspirants with colour vision issues, for obvious reasons. Safety is paramount and even in countries where the rules concerning corrective lenses have been relaxed, a pilot who is colour-blind can encounter difficulties when it comes to commanding a plane.

To begin with, a more politically correct term for colour blindness is colour vision deficiency (CVD) — the inability or a decreased ability to see and interpret colour correctly. About 8% of men and 0.5% of women are born colour-blind. That is as many as one in 12 men and one in 200 women.

There are various degrees of colour blindness. Protans are people who have problems recognising red while deutans are those who find it hard to identify green. The latter make up 99% of CVD cases. Red-green deficiency is the most common. Blue-yellow is next and is prevalent among three to six per cent of the world's population. This deficiency can arise from chemical exposure as well as the ageing of the eyes.

A person with colour deficiency is often slower to identify colours and more likely to misidentify them. This is why colour-blind people are restricted from becoming commercial pilots.

However, not all is lost if an aspiring pilot can pass a CVD test.

CRUCIAL COLOUR RECOGNITION

Colour vision is essential to pilots especially when flying at night. First, pilots must be able to recognise aircraft position lights. At night, it is easy for pilots with good vision to know if they are flying head-on towards another plane or safely in the same direction by merely looking at the lights on the other aircraft's wing tips.

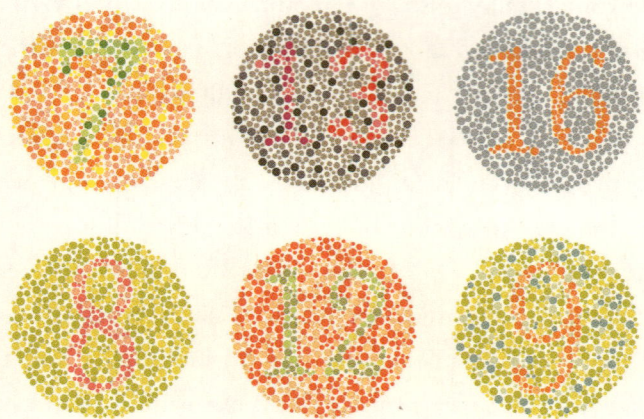

The Ishihara Colour Blindness Test: What do you see?

This is possible because the navigation light on the left wing tip is always red while that on the right wing tip is always green.

So, if you see a red light on the right and a green one on the left at night, this would mean you're on a collision course with the plane ahead!

Additionally, a pilot must be able to identify the colours of airport beacon lights, approach slope indicators, chart symbols and the light gun signal in an emergency. The light gun is used by air traffic control to communicate with aircraft, with different colours and flash patterns indicating specific directives.

But the most crucial signal to read is the approach slope indicator, a light system on the side of an airport runway threshold that provides visual descent guidance during approach. Its lights indicate whether a plane is well below the correct landing path (red) or too high (white) for a safe touchdown.

RUNWAY LIGHTS AND SAFETY

A pilot must also be able to distinguish the colours of runway lights during landing. For example, the green threshold lights at the beginning of the runway are of considerable significance when landing at night.

A colour-blind pilot might have difficulty perceiving a

displaced threshold — the part of the runway that cannot be used for landing because of its inability to sustain the continuous impact of landing aircraft — and land in the danger zone.

In extremely poor visibility, when visibility is restricted to about 100 metres, pilots may execute an automatic landing. But they are also trained to recognise the remaining runway length by distinguishing the colours of the runway centre line lights.

Variable white lights denote lots of room to spare, alternate red and white light indicate 3,000 feet to go, and red lights mean the pilot will run out of runway in another 1,000 feet.

Safety regulations state that a pilot must have the ability to perceive those colours for the safe performance of airman duties. An inability to satisfy this requirement may prohibit pilots from flying on grounds of colour deficiency.

COLOUR BLINDNESS TEST

An aspiring pilot with a mild case of colour blindness will have to pass a colour vision test. If he fails the test, he will be given a second chance with a different CVD check.

Most pilots with CVD are only mildly affected and can easily perceive the colours necessary for the safe performance of a flight. A person who has a significant and potentially

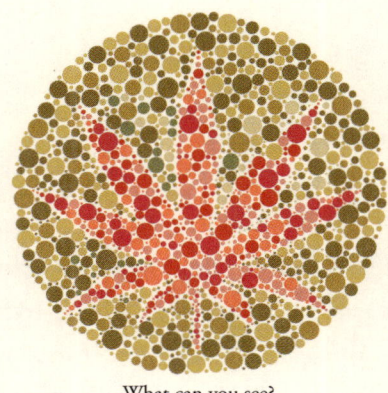

What can you see?

hazardous colour vision problem is likely to fail his colour vision examination.

CHALLENGE BY PILOT WITH CVD

In 1987, a pilot applicant in Queensland, Australia met all the requirements of his medical examination but was unable to meet the standards of the colour vision test. He was granted a licence, but with the condition that he not fly an aircraft at night. The pilot brought a case against the country's Civil Aviation Safety Authority requesting that his licence not be subject to that condition.

After many presentations by experts, it was decided that the pilot, a deutan, did not pose a significant and unacceptable risk to the public by flying an aircraft at all or at night simply because of his defective colour vision.

However, this case was an exception, and the pilot would require the approval of foreign civil aviation authorities if he were to operate outside Australia.

NOT THE END OF THE RUNWAY

I know a pilot with colour blindness who is flying as a first officer only because his medical test restricts him from exercising his privileges outside the Australian airspace or above his commercial pilot licence level, thereby precluding him from obtaining a command position and becoming a captain.

As you can see, an aspiring pilot with a mild case of CVD can still pursue his flying dream if he can satisfy some of the colour blindness tests, as prescribed by aviation doctors.

Chapter 27

COPING WITH JET LAG

Do pilots and cabin crew have special abilities that help them cope with jet lag? The answer is no. Pilots and cabin crew suffer just as much. Any traveller that crosses more than four time zones can expect to feel jet lag. However, if you know how to manage it, you can lessen its effects.

WHAT ARE THE TIME ZONES?

Before clocks were invented, timekeeping was done using the sun's shadow or with a water clock, an ancient device that measured time by the gradual flow of water.

Many early towns observed time based on sunset and sunrise, but this system was flawed. Dawn and dusk occurred at different times in different locations and the use of solar time became too unreliable to be of any use for the standardisation of time.

Time zones were not well set up and as such, early American railroads maintained more than 300 time zones according to the sun's position, making it difficult to coordinate train schedules. But this stopped when time zones were properly established. Since then, air travel has also adopted these time zones to have a uniform schedule for plane departures and arrivals worldwide.

THE START OF TIME ZONES

Greenwich, a town east of London in the UK, is used as the starting point for the calculation of longitude and time zones. Greenwich Mean Time (GMT) starts at 0.

Given that there are 24 hours in a day and 360 degrees of longitude around the earth, it is obvious that each of the world's one-hour time zones has to be 15 degrees or 900 nautical miles wide on average.

In reality, this is not so. In Malaysia, for example, although the distance between Kuala Lumpur and Tawau is more than 15 degrees in longitude and spans more than 1,000 nautical miles, the country has only one time zone (+8:00 GMT) for convenience of standardisation. Similarly, India (+5:30 GMT) and China (+8:00 GMT) both cover great distances from east to west, but have only one time zone, unlike other expansive countries such as the US, Russia, Australia and Indonesia.

Now that we understand time zones, let's see how it affects fatigue and jet lag. Pilots are not superhuman and jet lag affects them just as much as it does the average air traveller. This is why there are regulations in place to lessen its effects on those on duty.

The jet-lag effect of flying back to Malaysia from London is worse than when flying to London.

For instance, if pilots have to fly through many time zones, they are restricted to either a shorter working period or a longer rest period to ensure they are sufficiently rested before flying again.

CAUSES OF JET LAG

A tiny organ in the brain known as the pineal gland regulates your circadian rhythm (body clock) when you travel at great speeds over many time zones.

When light conditions are dim, the eye cells send a message to this gland, which releases a sleep-inducing hormone called melatonin, in response to the darkness. When you cross many time zones during your flight, your circadian system may not be in tune with the time of day at your destination. If daylight and darkness take place at times that your body is not used to, it will try to catch up with and resume the correct circadian rhythm, resulting in jet lag.

COMMON SYMPTOMS

Jet lag manifests through headaches, irritable behaviour, poor concentration and a whole lot of sleep issues such as poor and disrupted sleep upon arrival. It becomes worse if the traveller flies from west to east, towards a later time zone. Travelling from east to west will result in fewer jet-lag symptoms.

OVERCOMING JET LAG

There is no magic cure for jet lag except to reduce the severity of its effects. Some passengers take sleeping pills to get a little shut-eye and to mimic natural sleep rhythms, but this is not a cure for jet lag. Others believe that if they travel in first- or business-class comfort, they may escape jet lag. Of course, the perks you get in first class make your flight more comfortable but they don't do much for your body clock, which must still go through a readjustment period in the new time zone.

There is a general rule that one must allow a day's rest for every time zone crossed for the body clock to readjust. However, the rules for pilots are even more specific.

They must be given sufficient rest in order to prevent jet lag from affecting their flying performance. There are flight regulations in place to prevent pilots from being overly tired when flying through many time zones. These regulations define when a pilot becomes acclimatised or unacclimatised to a new destination.

Pilots are required to spend three nights at their destination when they fly across two time zones or more. For instance, when a pilot travels to London (+0:00 GMT) from Kuala Lumpur (+8:00 GMT), a time zone difference of eight hours, he is required to spend three local nights in London to acclimatise. If he spends only 24 hours in London, he is still unacclimatised and his subsequent flight duty period will be reduced.

TRAVELLING COMFORTABLY

In a nutshell, it is advisable not to smoke, consume alcohol or take unnecessary medication while flying. Sleep well before and during a long flight, consume small meals and drink plenty of fluids.

Jet lag affects anyone who travels across many time zones. In a new destination, the body must readjust and adapt to the new time zone. The process of readjustment manifests as jet lag and understanding the reasons behind it will definitely make air travel more pleasant.

Tips to beat jet lag
- Synchronise your watch by setting it to the local time of your destination as soon as possible to help your mind adjust to that time zone. You can also adapt faster to the time difference by eating and sleeping according to the time at your destination.
- Drink plenty of water during your flight. This is a common tip for general air travel. Some doctors recommend drinking at least two litres of water right before departure. You get dehydrated quite easily inflight owing to the dry cabin air. This results in diminished blood flow to your muscles and reduced kidney function, all of which induce jet lag.
- You can also choose to take melatonin capsules, as directed by a doctor. Melatonin is a sleep-inducing hormone that is naturally produced in the pineal gland.
- Exercise and consume food at the appropriate time.

Chapter 28
TRAVEL BUMPS

In 2014, an Airbus A330 flight from Kuala Lumpur to Brisbane had to make an emergency diversion to Bali, Indonesia because a pregnant passenger went into labour.

The airport manager at Bali was reported to have said that the plane had requested priority landing as the pregnant lady was "about to give birth". Upon landing, she was rushed to the hospital in an ambulance but it was too late to save the life of the newborn baby.

This incident gives rise to the often-asked question about what happens when a medical emergency crops up in the air. The good news is that these sorts of circumstances can be foreseen and thus, pilots and crew have been trained to handle them. Of course, the crew are not fully qualified medically and may request assistance in deciding whether or not to divert from someone on board who is better qualified.

The announcement requesting medical doctors on board to identify themselves to flight attendants may have been made popular through Hollywood movies and TV shows, but it happens in real life. Fortunately, there is someone to help most of the time.

IS IT SAFE TO FLY DURING PREGNANCY?

In the airline industry, medical emergencies contribute to more diversions than technical- or weather-related problems. Even though emergencies related to pregnancies are fairly uncommon, airlines have measures in place to manage them.

AirAsia's policy is quite clear. If the pregnancy is less than 28 weeks, the expectant mother is allowed to fly. But she will be required to sign a release and indemnity certificate to absolve the airline of any liability should anything unforeseen happen. If the pregnancy is between the 28th and 34th weeks, the expectant mother will need to obtain a medical certificate of at least one week's validity from her doctor stating the expected due date and her fitness to fly, in addition to signing the release and indemnity certificate.

Having complied with airline policy, pregnant women can travel, although it is strongly advised that they check with their obstetrician before flying. Generally, the best time to travel is during the middle three months of the pregnancy, or the second trimester (weeks 14 to 28), when the risk of miscarriage and premature labour is lowest.

The expectant mother should always choose an aisle seat and keep herself hydrated throughout the flight. She should avoid flying in unpressurised planes as the level of oxygen in the blood stream would be reduced. Flying at 10,000 feet is like standing on top of a mountain at 10,000 feet; the mother's body will have to work harder to provide sufficient oxygen for the baby she is carrying. Some passengers are concerned about cosmic radiation but this is not really an issue with short-haul air travel.

Security screening at the Departure gate in an airport.

SCREENING MACHINES AND X-RAYS

Metal detectors at security check points use very low frequency electromagnetic fields to identify hidden metal weapons. The levels of radiation emitted are very low, and the exposure is considered safe for pregnant women and other individuals. This is also true of the wands that security personnel sometimes pass over passengers.

Most people mistakenly believe that metal detectors use X-rays when, in fact, it is the luggage screeners that make use of X-rays to detect harmful objects. In airports in the US, there are now two new types of body-scanning machines. One uses low-level X-rays, which raises health concerns, while the other less controversial one uses electromagnetic waves.

TO DIVERT OR NOT TO DIVERT

Sometimes, the captain needs to decide whether or not to carry out a diversion. If he does not divert and a passenger dies, this would have negative repercussions and reflect badly on the airline. Hence, the captain has to seek the advice of a qualified medical professional, after verifying that that person is a doctor.

While medical diversion is an option, the decision to divert is weighed against the inconvenience caused to the other passengers, the cost involved and whether the sick person is better off with the support of family members and friends rather than being alone in a strange, unplanned destination. Making the decision even harder for the captain is the fact that sometimes there may not be any qualified medical personnel on board to assist him.

MEDICAL KITS AND TRAINING

The first aid kits on board are well-stocked and include defibrillators. A few big airlines have contracts with on-ground medical services that link the carriers to emergency specialists in major cities 24 hours a day.

Nevertheless, most inflight medical emergencies can usually be handled by the well-trained flight crew, with the assistance of any medical personnel on board. This is in compliance with current regulations. The US FAA requires that airline crew be trained to coordinate response to a medical emergency, use first aid kits and the automated external defibrillator and perform cardiopulmonary resuscitation (CPR).

The most common problems on board are dizziness and fainting, breathing difficulties and severe nausea and vomiting. Pregnancy-related problems are not very common but it has been found that most of these occur before the mother is 24 weeks pregnant. If you have a normal and healthy pregnancy, it can be perfectly safe to fly outside the cautionary period. However, it is always best to check with your doctor or obstetrician prior to your flight.

PART FIVE

PLANES AND HARDWARE

Chapter 29
TRAVELLERS' QUESTS

DOES A JET AIRCRAFT NEED TO CONSTANTLY ADJUST DOWN TO FOLLOW THE CURVATURE OF THE EARTH?

A plane will generally fly at a constant altitude and follow the curvature of the earth. It would not gain altitude during a level flight.

Two basic instruments, an altimeter and a vertical speed indicator (VSI), enable a plane to maintain a specific altitude. The VSI provides short-term changes in pressure and indicates whether the plane is climbing or descending, so the pilot can level the plane to maintain a level altitude, say, 35,000 feet. He would adjust the controls very slightly using the elevator and trims. Normally, this is performed by the autopilot. As such, the flight controls are constantly moving very subtly to maintain the correct attitude.

There is the assumption that if the plane was trimmed for a straight and level flight, it would gain altitude while in the sky owing to the curvature of the earth. This happens only in a perfectly motionless atmosphere, where the plane flies dead ahead and over time, gains altitude as the earth curves away from under the aircraft — provided it has sufficient thrust.

In reality, a constant altitude must be kept using the standard pressure and that means maintaining a fixed distance to the earth's centre of gravity, making the path of the plane a curved one. This is only obvious on very long flights.

ARE TWIN TURBOPROP ENGINES AS SAFE AS TWIN JET ENGINES?

There are some differences between twin turboprop and twin jet planes. A turboprop plane has a smaller jet engine to turn the propellers, whereas a jet engine has a bigger pure jet engine providing the thrust. Both basically have a jet engine.

A turboprop plane must not be confused with a plane that uses a piston engine to turn the propellers. (Turboprop engines are more reliable than piston engines, found in smaller planes such as the Cessna 172.)

Are twin turboprop planes as safe as jet planes?

My view is that both turboprop and jet engines are equally safe, although a turboprop plane has more moving parts, which increases the likelihood of mechanical issues. Nevertheless, if the engines are properly maintained, they are safe regardless of their type.

However, both types of engines can suffer from bird strikes. A small bird will just go through the engine and come out fried or vapourised. If the bird is of average-size, it may cause some damage to the engine. If it is large, like the Canada geese in the "Miracle on the Hudson" incident, it can cause severe damage to the engine.

Turboprops planes may be a little noisier but they are actually safer when landing on shorter runways. They are able to respond and stop much faster because the propellers provide extra drag and help the aircraft to stop when needed.

The other reason turboprops may be more suitable for certain routes is cost. Although jet planes are faster, for flights of less than 500 nautical miles, the additional time spent in the air is insignificant when compared with the fuel savings when you fly a turboprop.

DO AIRLINE PILOTS SUFFER FROM SUNBURN DURING LONG-HAUL FLIGHTS?

An aspiring pilot asked me whether flying, especially at high altitudes, can increase the risk of skin cancer. He also

observed that windshields in the cockpit are laminated and have a vinyl inter-layer to block out most types of ultraviolet rays, including both UVA and UVB.

It is true that airline pilots are more prone to UV radiation than the man in the street and, unfortunately, UV intensity does increase with altitude. This is part of the occupational hazard of being a pilot.

A study published in the *JAMA Dermatology* medical journal found that spending 56 minutes behind the controls in the cockpit at 30,000 feet is equivalent to spending 20 minutes stretched out on an average-strength sunbed.

The UV levels could be even higher when pilots fly over thick clouds and snow fields, which can reflect UV radiation.

Furthermore, airplane windshields do not completely block out UVA rays, which can pass through glass and penetrate the skin and eyes more deeply than UVB rays.

As such, pilots may be at increased risk of skin cancer because of frequent exposure to UV rays. That is why whenever I fly, I always pull down the cockpit window sunscreens to shield off the sunlight.

WHAT IS FLY-BY-WIRE?

When the Wright brothers first flew more than a century ago, their flight controls were fashioned from a unique idea known as wing warping. Wilbur and Orville Wright used a hip cradle to warp the wings of their Flyer. The wings were coupled to the rudder, and the tips could be twisted using a series of cables. The pilot shifts a simple wooden lever with his left hand to control the elevator in order to climb or descend.

Modern airliners no longer use wing warping to turn. They now employ ailerons, the moving sections on the wings.

When you next travel on a commercial plane, watch the wings during the turns. The pilot will roll the aircraft in the direction of the turn. You will probably be surprised to note how little deflection is necessary to turn a large airliner.

Gradually, as planes became larger, the heavier flight control surfaces had to be moved by cables and hydraulics. Today, cables have been replaced by the fly-by-wire (FBW) system.

THE FBW SYSTEM

"Wire" here refers to electrical signals. Prior to FBW, the flight controls of planes were connected to the pilots by physical cables, similar to those used to steer the rudder of a motorboat. For example, on old planes such as the Boeing 707, to commence a climb, the pilot would have to pull the flight control wheel up. This in turn moved the elevator control at the rear of the plane. This movement was possible because of cables. These cumbersome, lengthy and heavy cables are now replaced by electrical wires, reducing weight and thus saving cost. Hence the term "fly-by-wire".

The flight controls of the Boeing 777 are operated via the fly-by-wire system.

When a pilot intends to perform a climb on the Airbus A330, he gently pulls back the sidestick controller. The signal from the control is transmitted instantaneously to the elevators near the tail, not through cables but wires that run about 200 feet from the cockpit to the back.

As such, there are no direct mechanical links, cables or hydraulics between the pilots and control surfaces in the FBW system. This reduces the problem of removing cables, linkages and hydraulic tubing during maintenance. It also facilitates the use of software that can be incorporated into the autopilot system for safer flying.

The first flying machine to use the FBW concept successfully was the Apollo Lunar Module, in 1969. Apollo was able to take men from Earth's orbit to the surface of the moon. The landing of the rocket required a deftness and control that no human being could master then. The FBW concept was soon applied to new-generation military aircraft.

Even though the military had adopted FBW by the early 1980s, the commercial sector was less enthusiastic. The argument then was that commercial jets did not need the agility required to fly a fighter, nor did they have to worry about designing for stealth. But the fact is, FBW offered lower fuel costs as well as smoother flights in bad weather.

The Aérospatiale/BAC Concorde was the first FBW airliner, but this technology was slow to be introduced into commercial airlines until Airbus Industries did so in 1984, in its A320 airplanes. Ten years later, the Boeing Company followed suit with digital controls in its 777 planes. Thus, the FBW concept, basically the result of wanting to put man on the moon, has become an accepted part of modern aviation design.

BOEING'S PHILOSOPHY VERSUS AIRBUS'

Although the Boeing 777 and 787 and the Airbus A320, A330, A350 and A380 have adopted the FBW concept, there are slight differences in their applications. Airbus has taken a much different philosophical approach to using computers, designing its new FBW jets with built-in protections.

Boeing, on the other hand, believes pilots should have the ultimate say, and allows them to override onboard

Boeing Company's first fly-by-wire plane, the Boeing 777.

computers and their built-in limits, if necessary. The issue is should the pilot or a computer have ultimate control over a commercial jetliner as the plane approaches its design limits in an emergency?

There are strong arguments by pilots from both sides of the debate. Some are of the opinion that Airbus' computer protection is better whereas others support the Boeing philosophy that they should have the final say in controlling the airplane.

When the Airbus A320 first came out in 1987, it was marketed as a very safe plane. In other words, it was not possible to stall the plane in flight owing to a special inflight protection known as an alpha floor. When the plane approaches a predetermined attitude, the thrust levers will automatically apply full power to the engines to prevent the plane from falling off the sky.

However, an unfortunate accident happened shortly after the plane came onto the market during an air show in June 1988. An Airbus A320 crashed into the trees while making a low-and-slow fly-past in Habsheim, France. It was supposed to fly by with the gear down at about 100 feet. Instead, it came in at less than 30 feet off the ground. According to the captain, who survived the incident, there were issues with the radio altimeter and power acceleration which were not made known to them by the company.

Chapter 30

PLANES AND FUELS — SHARKLETS TO THE RESCUE

Ever wondered if putting jet fuel in your car would make it fly like a Formula One race car (or a plane)?

Unless you drive a diesel car, putting jet fuel in your tank will likely result in a stalled engine. That was what happened to several drivers in the US when they refuelled at a gas station in Keyport, New Jersey in 2012. Apparently, a fuel truck had wrongly delivered jet fuel instead of gasoline to that particular station.

Yet, some still think that using jet fuel in their cars would greatly enhance the vehicle's performance because a jet can cruise at around 500 miles per hour! Amusingly this is one of the myths surrounding jet fuel and aviation gas (avgas) used in piston-engine propeller planes.

The truth is, jet fuel is basically kerosene and is closer to regular diesel fuel. As such, you would be able to run it in a diesel car, although it would not lubricate the fuel system as a normal diesel fuel would.

On the other hand, smaller flying-club piston planes such as the Cessna 172 use avgas, which normally has a very high octane rating, often 100. You can use avgas for your car but it offers few advantages, such as stopping premature detonation (engine knocking), although that would require some modifications to the carburetor or injector settings.

AIRPLANE FUEL

Airplanes consume a lot of fuel; that is one of the reasons the supersonic Concorde was a commercial failure. An airline's survival, just like any other business, depends on making a profit, which, in the simplest terms, involves ensuring that costs do not exceed revenue.

However, with fuel prices escalating and ticket prices not rising in step owing to the abundance of low-cost carriers, many legacy airlines are on the verge of bankruptcy or have been forced to merge to stay afloat. Low-cost carriers find it easier to thrive because of their operating philosophy.

Airplane fuel is measured in kilograms or pounds, not litres or gallons, for obvious reasons. Weight is easier to work with in flying. For instance, I would make a request for 50,000kg of fuel to fly to Melbourne from Kuala Lumpur on an Airbus A330 instead of 16,202 gallons. This is because it is easier for me to work out the weight restrictions, such as whether the plane can take off safely without exceeding the maximum allowable take-off weight.

Let's look at this from another angle. A Boeing 747 consumes about five gallons of fuel for every mile flown. This looks very bad compared to the 25 miles per gallon achieved by some cars on the road today. However, if you consider that a 747 can carry 500 passengers on each flight, it actually gets four times better mileage per passenger versus a single-passenger car. In the bigger Airbus A380, which can carry a maximum of about 800 passengers and boasts fuel consumption that is comparable to the 747, the figures would be even more impressive!

Fuel makes up about 30% to 40% of an airline's operating costs. That is why most airlines are very conscious of fuel-saving.

The story making its way around social media is that to save fuel, pilots from an Australian airline flying the Airbus A380 super jumbos were being asked, if possible, to carry minimum fuel on long-haul flights. Apparently, as a result, at least two flights were forced to divert because of fuel issues, although the airline insisted there were other reasons for the diversion.

So, do pilots take sufficient fuel for a particular flight and how do they determine how much to take?

A TYPICAL AIRLINE FUEL POLICY

Let me explain the fuel planning policy of a typical flight and how conservativeness is factored into the fuel uplift to comply with international regulations.

For a typical flight, say, from Kuala Lumpur to Melbourne, the total fuel carried would consist of the trip fuel plus a certain percentage for contingency. On top of this, there must be enough extra fuel to redirect to an alternate aerodrome and hold at this airport for an additional 30 minutes in the event of an unforeseen air traffic delay. Some airports have long taxiways, which means the plane has to spend more time on the ground. This, too, has to be taken into account. And finally, the captain can carry any extra discretionary fuel he considers necessary in anticipation of an approaching storm, or snow or fog.

HOW AIRLINES PRACTISE FUEL-SAVING

Airlines strive to save fuel and initiate many steps towards that. One simple step is similar to a driving tip: Remove unnecessary heavy items in the trunk or back seat to reduce fuel consumption. The aviation equivalent of this is captured in the saying, "The heavier you are, the more fuel you will burn." As such, removing unnecessary items such as galley tables and magazine racks from the cabin, reducing water uplift for short sectors as well as taking only necessary fuel for the flight would be the smart order of the day.

Pilots have been trained to fly a plane efficiently with minimum drag during approach to land, to delay the auxiliary power unit start-up and to use minimum reverse thrust consistent with safety after landing. Such are the fuel-saving measures being encouraged.

SHARKLETS

New wingtip devices such as the Airbus A320 Sharklets also help increase fuel efficiency. Sharklets, so named because of their resemblance to a shark's dorsal fin, were inspired by large birds such as the crane, which curl their wingtip feathers upward. They greatly improve aircraft energy efficiency when flying and allow for a steeper climb angle, which reduces noise emissions in the vicinity of an airport.

Sharklets also enhance the amount of cargo the A320 can carry by up to 450kg, and increase its performance by adding an extra 100 nautical miles to its range.

Sharklets on the wing tip of an Airbus A320neo.

RUNNING OUT OF FUEL

On Jan 25, 1990, a Boeing 707 operated by Spanish airline Avianca ran out of fuel and crashed at JFK International Airport. It had been in a holding pattern for over one hour because of a heavy thunderstorm and wind interfering with smooth arrivals and departures at the airport. While waiting for the weather to improve, the aircraft exhausted its reserve fuel supply that would have allowed it to divert to its alternate airport in Boston.

The accident investigation board determined that the main cause of the accident was pilot error as the captain never declared a fuel emergency to the ATC. Apparently, one of the causes cited for this incident was language difficulties, including not using the proper terms when communicating distress.

Normally, once the crew has about 30 minutes of flying time left, they would declare to the control tower that they have minimum fuel. The ATC will acknowledge such calls because if further delays are imposed, it would lead to an emergency. As such, a "Mayday" call repeated three times would be made when an aircraft has less than 30 minutes endurance left. In such instances, immediate landing clearance would be given to the plane. In the Avianca incident, the Spanish captain did not declare the "Mayday!" call, which would have made the difference.

CARBON FOOTPRINT

The aviation industry has been a convenient scapegoat for climate change, with claims that airlines produce an obscene amount of carbon compared with other forms of travel. However, this argument does not hold water when you consider the fuel burned by a plane on a per passenger basis compared with driving an automobile.

Knowing what you know now, you will understand that

the pilot would have carefully plotted out the optimum amount of fuel to carry to transport you safely to your destination. It is a fine balancing act, but we do it on a daily basis, so much so that it has become second nature. So rest easy and fly safely!

Chapter 31
MACHINE VERSUS MAN

A reader wrote to me specifically to find out about pilotless cargo planes of the future. I explained that in the future, pilotless planes would not be confined to cargo but be able to fly commercial fare-paying passengers as well. It is only a question of time.

UNMANNED FLIGHTS

This change in the aviation scene could start with having only one pilot in the cockpit, and then none at all. The "pilot" would probably be someone on the ground performing certain flight duties, like NASA's mission control centre.

This is precisely how the unmanned aerial vehicles (UAV) or drones currently being used by the US military are operated. In fact, in 2001, a UAV from the Edwards Air Force Base in California flew for 24 hours with no humans in the cockpit, before touching down safely at an air base in Edinburgh, South Australia.

CONDITIONS FOR PILOTLESS AIRLINERS

For pilotless planes to become a reality, at least three conditions must be satisfied. A safe pilotless plane must first be built, then there must be a good enough reason to use such a plane. Finally, but most importantly, passengers must be willing to fly in one.

Well, safe pilotless planes are not too far from reality. The main hurdle that needs to be cleared is more commercial viability, as opposed to feasibility. A pilotless plane would require more costly equipment on the runway to be developed for automated take-off. At this point in time, the cost of such a venture outweighs the benefits. As it is, the process of taking off manually is much easier than engaging in an automated one.

A very good reason for using pilotless planes would be economics. Compared with other professions, a pilot's salary is among the highest in the world because of the costly training required to license a pilot. Market forces are also a critical factor in determining the salary level, as well as the fact that there aren't many professions that are responsible for so many lives.

Pilots are human and may possibly make mistakes, whereas machines do not get tired and are extremely accurate when properly programmed.

Nowadays, no one blinks an eye when taking a lift or train that is not manned. A time will come when people will accept that flying in pilotless planes is just like using a lift. The likely scenario in the future is that cargo aircraft will be used to test the feasibility of pilotless planes. This will give the public confidence that it is perfectly safe to have unmanned cargo planes carrying freight from point A to B. Low-cost carriers keen on further reducing costs may follow suit before legacy airlines finally jump on the bandwagon.

The main issue would be the public's acceptance of being flown by computers. Nevertheless, the day will come when passengers will have to accept that computers will be in charge in the air. I can only say that this will likely not happen in my lifetime, or that of the next generation.

REPLACING PILOTS

This idea of being replaced appears to have caused some anxiety among aspiring pilots. One asked whether he should pursue a flying career at all.

Future planes will not have cockpits. Airlines of the future may have planes that only have a few "pilots" and systems engineers on the ground to link them to the airborne airliners electronically.

An aircraft commander of the future would probably be the purser, the most senior cabin crew member in the air, who will be assisted by other crew in managing the passengers. So, even though the plane may be pilotless, it will still be manned by the head of the cabin staff.

Another good reason to replace man with machine is that the latter tends to be more reliable. This would greatly eliminate pilot error. For instance, accidents such as that of Air France Flight 447 in 2009, which was attributed to pilot error, would not have happened.

RELYING ON AUTOMATION

Today, the immediate concern is that most pilots are so accustomed to automation and rely too much on computers, to the extent that they are gradually losing their manual flying skills. This is just like an accountant relying on his computer to do all the accounting work, to the detriment of basic calculating skills.

The rationale of airlines in recommending more automation is that it provides greater comfort to passengers and saves fuel. Fuels of the future will be extremely expensive. As of now, cost has killed the fuel-guzzling Concorde.

When I first began flying many years ago, there was no automation in my first plane, the de Havilland Canada DHC-4 Caribou. It was a manual operation, which could become extremely tiring especially as I had to fly a seven-hour stretch on a plane that cruised at one-third the speed of current jet planes. Passengers also had to endure the discomfort of a rough journey owing to the pilot constantly adjusting to the correct altitude and heading manually, which also burnt extra fuel in the process.

After the Air France Flight 447 crash, which had 228 fatalities, investigations revealed that the pilots lacked the basic flying skills to recover from a high-altitude stall caused by unreliable airspeed indications. Hence, the recommendation was to go back to basics with more manual flying training for all pilots.

It is a fact that humans can never fly as accurately as the autopilot. The disclaimer is that the automation and computers must be accurately managed and programmed in order to ensure perfection.

Many passengers are unaware that in extremely poor weather conditions with almost zero visibility, they would not have reached their destination safely if it were not for computers. Pilots are physically in the cockpit only to monitor and manage the auto-landing system and to take over and abort the landing in case of an emergency, something that could be easily replicated by computers in the future.

CHANGING REALITY

As you can see, pilotless planes are not too far from reality. Airliners would be controlled by systems managers on the ground and aviation technology of the future would be so advanced that the unthinkable would be the accepted norm.

An industry joke has it that the plane of the future would only require a pilot and a dog. Why do we need a dog in the cockpit? Well, she is there to bark at the captain when he selects the wrong button. And the pilot's last remaining job would be to feed the dog!

Chapter 32
THE GLASS COCKPIT

Recently, I visited Nepal to experience life in the Roof of the World. Tribhuvan International Airport in Kathmandu is one of the most exciting airports in the world. Flying an approach into the valley and onto the runway at 4,400 feet above sea level in cloudy weather is certainly an unusual experience. Only dedicated airline pilots who are trained and competent are permitted to fly to this destination because of its difficult approach, especially during bad weather.

A spectacular view of Mount Everest in Nepal.

A UNIQUE APPROACH

Why is the approach into Tribhuvan unique for big airliners? Well, it is a "one way in, one way out" airport owing to the high terrain to the north of the airfield. Bigger planes require more room to manoeuvre in the event of an engine failure. Hence, the stringent procedures imposed for safety reasons by certain airlines.

To fly into Tribhuvan, initially, pilots must approach the runway from the south, staying high then dipping steeply to perform a challenging landing in the bowl-shaped city of Kathmandu. Not only must the pilot stay high, he must also maintain the runway approach centre line. On any given cloudy day, isolated thunderstorms sit smack in the centre path.

Any deviation at this point would bring the plane very close to mountainous terrain. Hence, the approach to land is often a rather rough ride on such days as the pilot has very little choice but to charge through the storm clouds for a short while.

VIEWS OF EVEREST

A traveller to this city would often be harassed by travel agents promoting fly-bys to Mount Everest. Not surprisingly, I was instantly approached by an agent and handed a leaflet touting a spectacular Everest flight that offers tourists who are unable to climb the mountain a breathtaking view of its peak. Of course, being an aviator myself, I knew that at the time of my visit, the peak would likely be shrouded in clouds.

There were three airlines offering the Everest flight experience and something that may have easily been missed by non-pilots caught my eye. One airline proudly extolled a British Aerospace Jetstream plane that could make a traveller's Everest experience "as reliable as possible" with its full-glass cockpit and Enhanced Ground Proximity Warning System (EGPWS), among others.

This may be misleading advertising, as it implies that you will be flown in a transparent flying device to fully experience the magnificent marvels of Mount Everest. Unfortunately, this is not quite true. A glass cockpit is not really a space enclosed by glass that allows a pilot to see through all around him. It is not like looking out of a bottle from the inside.

THE GLASS COCKPIT

In the past, one would see mechanical gauges and traditional analogue dials on the instrument panels of cockpits. Today, modern aircraft feature electronic instruments with digital displays. This enables data from the flight management system to be shown on LCD screens.

Such screens and the earlier cathode ray tube displays are basically made of glass, hence the term glass cockpit. By using

The flight instruments in a glass cockpit.

computers to manage the flight in a glass cockpit, pilots are able to call up what they want to see, when they want to see it. The advancement in this technology has effectively reduced the need for flight engineers. Planes that used to have three crew members in the cockpit now require only two — a captain and a first officer — which translates into huge savings.

On the flip side, these technological advancements place a greater burden on pilots inside the glass cockpit. For instance, the glass cockpit concept might have confused the pilots of a British Midland Boeing 737-400 on Jan 8, 1989. A fan blade in one of the engines had failed but the crew, guided by the display in the glass cockpit, proceeded to shut down the remaining good engine as well. It was basically the confusing display of earlier systems, which were often misread, that caused the error in identifying the proper engine. Fortunately, pilot information has been improved with a better display system, thus minimising erroneous readings.

On Jan 20, 1992, Air Inter's Airbus A320 with glass cockpit technology flew into a mountain on a night approach to Strasbourg, France, all because the pilot operated a knob erroneously. This knob allows the flight instruments in a glass cockpit to switch between degrees and rate of descent when commanding the aircraft to descend. The pilots thought they had commanded the plane to descend at an angle of 3.2 degrees, but they had actually instructed the plane to begin a 3,200-feet-per-minute descent — a far steeper rate. After this, Airbus redesigned the descent mode display in its glass cockpit.

EGPWS SAVES LIVES

EGPWS (Enhanced Ground Proximity Warning System) is an improvement over the traditional GPWS (Ground Proximity Warning System) that had some limitations. GPWS works off an aircraft's radar altimeter, a very accurate sensor of how high the plane is above the ground, but only up to 2,500 feet, as opposed to a normal barometric altimeter, which is accurate up to 50,000 feet.

When the GPWS senses that the aircraft is getting dangerously close to the ground, it alerts the crew. However, since the radar altimeter looks straight down and not in front of the aircraft, it does not give any warning when encountering very steep terrain, such as a vertical rock face.

THE PERILS OF WHITEOUT

The EGPWS addresses this shortcoming. It can look ahead of the aircraft and detect a potential collision with terrain. This system, sadly, was not available in 1979 when a McDonnell Douglas DC-10 belonging to Air New Zealand crashed into Mount Erebus in the South Pole. Investigations revealed that the main cause of the disaster was the crew's inability to see rising terrain ahead, namely Mount Erebus, and their not having sufficient visual warning.

The crew had suffered a whiteout, a condition in which visibility and contrast ahead of the pilot are severely reduced by snow. The horizon disappears completely and there are no reference points at all. This causes the pilots to have a distorted orientation because of the continuous white cloud layer appearing to merge with the white snow surface. Hence, there is no visible horizon, to the extent that a pilot may not even know he is flying inverted unless he looks at the instruments.

How come the crew of the DC-10 did not see the mountain ahead? Well, they were unable to distinguish between the cloud base and the rising terrain until it was too late. If an EGPWS was available then, it would have alerted the crew with this warning: "Terrain! Terrain! Pull Up!" That would have saved the day.

BEST TIME FOR KATHMANDU

If you are planning a trip to this mountainous country, the best time to visit would be from December to April. These months denote the drier season when the skies are clearer, which will give you a better view of the amazing peaks. Flying over the mountainous terrain in a glass cockpit would be a great experience, as long as you don't expect the plane to be fully transparent!

Chapter 33
BLOWS AND BIRDS

SUCK, SQUEEZE, BANG AND BLOW

On a plane, the component responsible for the "suck" function is the fan in the engine intake. This can pull in a large volume of air and direct it to the compressor, which does the "squeezing". More on that later!

Big birds flying close to the plane may make a pretty picture, but they could cause lots of trouble.

A typical commercial jet engine sucks in 1,200kg of air per second during take-off. In other words, it could empty the air in a squash court in less than a second! At lower power, the suction can be very lethal too. It can suck in anything located near the front of the engine, be it humans (one mechanic at Texas in 2006), cargo containers, traffic cones or other objects.

The compressor "squeezes" the incoming air through a series of spinning blades in stages. The more stages there are, the higher the compression ratio and hence, its efficiency. For example, if the compression ratio is 40:1, it means the pressure of the air at the end is over 40 times that of the air entering the compressor.

The "bang" is produced inside the combustion chamber. Very simply, the combustor is just like a butane cigarette lighter. The compressed air is ignited here. Gases that form expand rapidly, get exhausted and are blown through the rear of the combustion chambers, creating thrust, typically 110,000 pounds of force in some jet engines.

The piston engine in your car has a similarly simplistic explanation: suck, squeeze, burn and blow, with "burn" replacing the "bang". In a car, the final effect of the process turns the crankshaft, ultimately moving the wheels. On a jet engine, the final effect of "blow" is the thrust, similar to the force of releasing the air in a balloon, causing it to zoom away.

POWER OF JET SUCTION

Now that you know the enormous suction power of the jet engine, never, never stray towards a live jet engine!

To prevent costly damage to jet engines, airlines and aviation authorities put many precautions in place. Among them, the manoeuvring area of the plane from the moment it moves from the parking position to the take-off runway has to be spotlessly maintained to prevent debris from being ingested by the engines.

The runways and parking aprons are regularly checked to ensure they are free from pieces of broken concrete, materials from cabin-cleaning, wheels dislodged from luggage, tools and bolts unwittingly left behind by mechanics, and other unwanted items. Even small objects can sometimes cause catastrophic damage if sucked into an engine. As part of stringent testing for all new planes, the US FAA requires that all new engine designs must pass a test that includes withstanding the firing of a chicken carcass into a running engine using a small cannon. This test must not affect the operation of the plane.

In 2000, an Air France Concorde crashed at Charles de Gaulle International Airport in Paris. This incident, the Concorde's only fatal accident in its 27-year operational history, was caused by a piece of metal debris that fell off a Continental Airlines McDonnell Douglas DC-10 plane which had taken off four minutes earlier. This highlights the need for diligent debris removal from the runway and its surrounding areas.

BIG BIRDS, MAJOR HAZARD

Large birds are also considered dangerous flying objects to aircraft engines. On Nov 20, 1975, a Hawker Siddeley HS 125 taking off at Dunsfold aerodrome south of London flew through a flock of birds after lifting off and lost power in both the engines.

The crew landed the aircraft back on the runway, but it overran the end and crossed a road. The aircraft struck a car on the road, killing its six passengers.

On Nov 17, 1980, a Hawker Siddeley Nimrod jet crashed shortly after taking off from a Royal Air Force station north of Scotland. It flew through a flock of Canada geese, causing three of its four engines to fail.

REDUCING BIRD STRIKE THREATS

Bird strikes account for more than two strikes per 10,000 aircraft movements and are becoming even more frequent. Wilbur Wright was the first pilot to record a bird strike in 1905, but the most newsworthy one was caused by the geese that downed Captain Sully's Airbus A320.

A bird detection system known as BirdWize was launched

in 2013 to reduce bird strikes by making the tracking of ground-level birds more effective.

ERADICATING LOOSE OBJECTS

Damage from loose objects, known in aviation as foreign object damage or FOD, costs the industry about US$13 billion in direct and indirect costs every year.

To prevent FOD, sweeping is carried out before flight operations begin. You may sometimes see a line of personnel walking shoulder-to-shoulder along open surfaces searching for and removing loose objects.

The FAA and the International Civil Aviation Organization (ICAO) require a daily, daylight inspection of airplane manoeuvring areas and removal of loose objects.

PREEMPTING DAMAGE

Flying is safe because the airline industry takes a lot of effort to eradicate costly damage caused by loose objects on the ground and in the air.

On Nov 15, 2013, Boston Logan International Airport became the first airport in the US to install a system that automates the job of identifying objects which may damage an aircraft during take-off or landing.

So, be kind and proactive. You, too, can also participate in flight safety. Pick up any loose objects such as shoe studs or a metal nut that you come across as you make your way to the plane on an open tarmac. You could save lives through that small, conscientious act.

Chapter 34
SECRET REVEALED

ALL IN THE BOX

On Sept 8, 2010, a Boeing 737-800 flying from Dubai in the United Arab Emirates to Mangalore, India crashed while carrying out a tricky landing in the Indian city's table-top airport — so dubbed for the deep surrounding gorges that leave no room for error and make it especially difficult for pilots to land and take off during the rainy season.

Investigators determined that the pilot had been sleeping prior to the crash. How did they know this? The black box had the answer. The details, including the sound

The black box is usually a bright orange as it is intended to be spotted easily.

of the pilot snoring in the cockpit, were captured by its voice recorder.

Although the pilot's falling asleep did not directly cause the Mangalore air crash, it showed he was tired and might not have prepared well for the flight that eventually ended in a fatal accident.

IN THE BEGINNING…

During an air crash investigation, the black box is often mentioned by the media. Investigators are always very keen to know if it has been recovered so that they will be able to find out the cause of an accident.

The black box was first invented by a young Australian scientist who was involved in the investigation of the mysterious crash in 1954 of the world's first jet plane, the de Havilland Comet. In 1960, Australia became the first country to make the installation of the black box mandatory after an unexplained crash in Queensland involving a Fokker Friendship airliner in the same year.

However, the origin of the term "black box" is uncertain. One explanation dates back to World War II, when metal boxes containing electronic innovations were added to bomber planes as part of the war strategy. These boxes were painted black to prevent reflection. They were referred to as a "box of tricks" or "black box" back then.

After the war, the expression continued to be used in civil aviation. In reality, the black box is not black but usually bright orange, so that it can be spotted easily and recovered after an air accident. The term is more often used by the media and almost never technically in the flight safety industry. By regulation, this crucial device must be installed on all commercial aircraft and corporate jets today.

The black box contains a cockpit voice recorder (CVR) and a flight data recorder (FDR). The first device records what the crew says and monitors any sound that occurs within the cockpit. In the beginning, the US FAA requirement was that the last recording should be at least 30 minutes, but today, the duration has been extended to two hours.

The FDR records the different flight data of a plane all at once, such as the time, altitude, airspeed and the direction in which the plane is heading. This information is very important as it helps investigators figure out what happened before an accident.

LOCATING THE BLACK BOX

How would investigators locate the black box in the ocean in the aftermath of a plane crash? Each recorder has a device known as an underwater locator beacon fitted to it. The locator is activated and starts transmitting as soon as the

All cockpit inflight data is recorded by the black box.

recorder is contaminated with water. The transmitter can send distress signals from as deep as 14,000 feet.

The recorders are very durable and capable of withstanding temperatures of up to about 1,000 degrees Celsius for one hour, or 260 degrees Celsius for 10 hours.

You might wonder why then are planes not built to black box standards. Well, because they would be so heavy you would have to drive them rather than fly in them!

INFLIGHT TELEMETRY

Why do modern planes still make use of the black box when global satellite technology is capable of doing away with it, especially when inflight telemetry, or the constant broadcasting of remote data to the ground, has been used so widely in modern car races?

With inflight telemetry, there would be no risk of the voice and data recorders being lost, especially in the ocean, in the event of an accident. It would probably also mean that far more data could be sent back, compared with the limited storage capacity offered by the black box.

A reader noted that the motor sports circle has been beaming real-time telemetry from cars for years. He was working in the technology industry and said this was not beyond the realm of current possibility, and it seemed like such an obvious thing to do.

LIVE BLACK BOX

After the immense cost and time involved in recovering the black box of the Air France Airbus A330 which plunged into the Atlantic Ocean in 2009, the live black box was touted as the solution for future air-crash investigations. Subsequently, Airbus announced that it would begin studying a system to transmit flight data via air-to-ground links in a commercially viable way.

There are many reasons the "live black box" inflight telemetry data system should be installed in all modern planes, with the exception of the hefty implementation cost, which has to be borne by the airlines.

Data storage is not an issue but data bandwidth is, especially on satellites that would be required to cover the oceanic areas and the poles. It would cost about US$1 per kilobyte. This would be a running cost, much like fuel and maintenance, as opposed to a one-off charge at the initial outlay when purchasing a plane. Because of the competitive nature of the aviation industry, most airlines would be reluctant to invest in inflight telemetry and dilute their profit, unless it was made mandatory.

Inflight telemetry, when perfected, would also be useful in saving planes in distress. It would require that the system be capable of detecting when a plane is in trouble. Detailed information could be linked to a pilot or engineer standing by on the ground, who would receive data and communicate with the pilots on board — just like the NASA mission control!

AIR TRANSAT FUEL LEAK

In August 2001, an Air Transat Airbus A330 suffered a fuel leak that resulted in the loss of both engines. It was fortunate that the crew was able to save the plane by gliding it to land safely in the Azores, Portugal. All 306 people on board were safe and the plane was undamaged except for some burst tyres. In this case, it was humans that aggravated the accident. The crew had tried to balance the fuel level by pumping fuel from the heavy tank to the leaking one. By doing so, they unconsciously depleted the total fuel on board, resulting in both engines failing.

An experienced individual observing the same fuel data might have been able to detect the mistake earlier. In this sense, a streaming data link would be useful.

KNOWLEDGE FOR THE FUTURE

The importance of the recovery of the Air France black box was fundamental. When it was finally recovered from the ocean about two years after the disaster, it enabled the investigators to determine precisely what caused it and make recommendations to prevent future accidents. To overcome the delay in retrieving the data, continuous data streaming would appear to be the answer.

This safety innovation is highly feasible; it will merely be an improvement on the "live black box" telemetry technology. Planes in distress can also make use of this technology to activate "mission control" for help when their internal resources are lacking.

The technology for inflight telemetry is available. It is

now down to governments and regulators to make it a law and mandate that this be done. Until then, the current black box technology is still viable, and it does the job. It is just not live or streaming.

PART SIX
WEATHER

Chapter 35
WEATHERING OBSTACLES

Flying has come a long way since the Wright brothers first flew the Kitty Hawk in 1903. Many issues on weather that once affected flight safety have since been understood and addressed.

Aircraft are much better equipped and good flying techniques are constantly being introduced to ensure that passengers travel in utmost safety and comfort.

Pilots take great pains to plan every flight, as carefully as if their very own families were on board. Prior to

Flying above the clouds is less turbulent than inside.

every departure, the captain and his first officer will run through a series of briefings, especially on how to manage threats or deal with errors with regards to the weather for the day.

When I was flying, I would first check if my flight would encounter turbulence or thunder clouds (cumulonimbus), or whether there would be any rain or poor visibility which could potentially hamper my landing.

HANDLING TURBULENCE

Turbulence is a common topic discussed by air travellers. A plane flying in the air is just like an ocean liner at sea. When the sea is rough, the ship will rock. Similarly, a plane will shake on encountering turbulent air.

There is nothing for passengers to worry about as long as they have their seat belts securely fastened. In fact, the captain would generally know in advance that he will be approaching an unavoidable patch of irregular air mass.

Visually, he would know that the rocky ride would soon affect his plane and he would try his best to manoeuvre away from the turbulent air.

A pilot can also check the smoothness of his journey by reviewing the route forecast on the flight plan, as every segment of his flight would have an indication of the severity of turbulence the plane would encounter, known as shear rate.

Shear rate ranges from a figure of 0 to 20, and anything rated five upwards is a warning to the captain to be on his toes.

Depending on the ride, he may caution passengers by switching on the seat belt sign. Prior to encountering the "roller coaster ride", he would reduce his speed just like a motorist approaching a speed bump on the road would.

Turbulence is normal. It may, at times, cause the wing tips of the aircraft to flex a little and the engines to shake slightly on the pylon. But they are designed to do so. Structurally, the wings of most modern planes are very strong and are constructed to withstand about 150% of the strongest force that the plane can encounter in flight.

AVOIDING THUNDERSTORMS

Thunderclouds are shown on the radar screen of the plane as red at its most intense spot and pilots avoid them like the plague. Flying in their vicinity would make for a choppy ride and lightning strikes become a possibility.

Depending on the height of the plane and the clouds, the captain may request deviation of around 20 nautical miles to stay clear of turbulence associated with these clouds. However, lightning in the vicinity of a thunderstorm, though fearsome, is generally not dangerous to the airplane or its passengers. Even if there is a direct strike, it will not penetrate the cabin. Modern airliners are built to absorb over eight times the energy carried by a bolt of lightning. When an airplane is struck, the electrical charges just traverse the length of the aircraft and exit through static dischargers at the trailing edges of the flaps or tailplane. I have personally experienced lightning strikes on my plane when flying and treated it as a routine occurrence. I merely reported the encounter to the engineer upon landing.

NAVIGATING WITH POOR VISIBILITY

Poor visibility is a factor to be considered for safe landing. A well-trained flight crew will be able to land an aircraft even in very poor visibility of 100 metres, using the ILS, a highly accurate and dependable system that is fully capable of guiding an airplane to a runway in poor weather conditions. For airports without ILS, visibility has to be good for a pilot to attempt landing.

The conventional wisdom among pilots is that they should not attempt a third landing once they have tried twice to land in poor visibility without the aid of the ILS. Instead, they should divert to another airport. Statistics have proven that doing otherwise is ill-advised.

FLYING IN THE RAIN

Rain may reduce visibility during take-off or landing. Commercial airliners have strict rules about weather conditions, including minimum visibility. There are operational limitations. For instance, I have refused to take off in the rain with crosswinds during an approaching typhoon, a decision that incurred the ire of some passengers. Such actions are taken with the safety of passengers in mind.

Passengers are quite delighted when a landing is smooth. That usually happens on a good day when the runway is dry. However, landing smoothly is not necessarily desirable all the time. When the runway is wet, a firm, positive touchdown

or landing is necessary in order to prevent aquaplaning. Too smooth a landing will fool the computer into believing that the plane has not landed and the anti-skid system operation may not kick in. Advanced avionics and computerisation have made it possible to land in low visibility without much fuss.

COOL IN THE COCKPIT

While you might imagine that the cockpit crew are working furiously when the plane is encountering turbulence, the truth is that your pilot is probably wondering if there are any passengers who may have forgotten to buckle up when the seat belt sign is switched on. To the flight crew, turbulence is a normal part of flying.

The wings and body structure of a plane are incredibly strong and can withstand very strong pressure exerted on them. Even in very poor visibility, auto landing will safely deliver you to your destination.

Chapter 37
BUMPS IN THE AIR

Some air travellers describe their encounter with air pockets as dropping thousands of feet.

I have often explained that the experience is similar to travelling on land when a smooth road suddenly gives way to bumps and potholes, making the journey a little uncomfortable.

WHAT IS AN AIR POCKET?

Despite the term being quoted so often, it is in fact impossible for there to be a "pocket" in the sky as air vacuums cannot exist in the atmosphere.

The term "air pocket" was allegedly invented by a journalist who was covering World War I from an aircraft. It is assumed that he was referring to the jostling of the plane and attributed the cause to "pockets of air" while he was flying around. The expression caught on and travellers still refer to turbulence as air pockets.

OVERCOMING TURBULENCE

Let me replace the term "air pockets" with "turbulence" —

which is almost impossible to avoid on most long-haul flights and even some short-haul trips. Pilots do their best to steer clear of the conditions that cause turbulence by deviating from the aircraft's predetermined route and climbing or descending. However, there are still times when the aircraft may experience unavoidable turbulence.

THE SCIENCE BEHIND IT

According to Captain Tom Bunn, a therapist, pilot and the founder of SOAR, a programme designed to help those with a fear of flying, turbulence is the number one problem among people who are afraid to fly. According to his research, what people see is the inside of the aircraft and they imagine it being vulnerable high up in the sky as nothing is holding it up. Though their rational brain may understand that air can hold the plane up, their emotional brain needs to see it to believe it. Since the emotional brain, which is primarily visual, cannot see anything holding the plane up, it cannot comprehend how the plane remains in the air.

If you were to lose your balance and fall off a stepladder, the amygdala, the part of your brain that releases stress hormones, would zap you with them to make you aware of the situation. When the plane drops in altitude during turbulence, the amygdala reacts in the same way.

Always buckle up during turbulence.

It would be okay if the turbulence consisted of just one drop. But turbulence means one drop after another and you get bombarded with stress hormones. When these build up, the ability to think normally decreases. This is something akin to temporary schizophrenia. Whatever you have in your mind is accepted as real and a drop of a few feet feels a lot more dramatic!

HOW YOUR BRAIN REACTS

There are two types of memory cells in your brain — quick-learning and slow-learning. When two incidents happen at the same time or in quick succession, the quick-learning cells link them together. But if the first incident happens several times without the second happening, the quick-learning cells do a quick relearning and unlink the two incidents.

The slow-learning cells, on the other hand, need the two incidents to happen at the same time or in quick succession several times before they link them in the mind. After that, if the two incidents stop happening together, the slow-learning cells are slow to relearn that there is no connection between them.

During a trauma, both the quick- and slow-learning cells treat the situation as life-threatening. If the situation is repeated a few times and nothing traumatic happens, the quick-learning cells accept that. This, however, is not the case with the slow-learning cells. They refuse to accept that what once was convincingly life-threatening is now not so.

What does this tell us about turbulence? Once you have been in turbulence and believed you were in a precarious situation, the slow-learning cells will continue — although not as strongly as at first — to react to turbulence.

This, I believe, explains why no matter how much I try to reassure guests that turbulence is not a safety problem, anxious fliers who have experienced rough turbulence still fear it.

> **DID YOU KNOW?**
> Aircraft rarely experience dramatic drops in altitude as the autopilot is in control most of the time.
>
> Airplanes experience turbulence because they are moving under their own power against the atmosphere. In hot air balloons, there is no turbulence because they flow with the wind, not push against it.
>
> Turbulence has been given nicknames such as "roller coaster ride", "spiller of coffee" and "rattler of nerves".

Chapter 38

WINDS BENEATH YOUR WINGS

There are different kinds of winds that aid or encumber aircraft on the ground and in the air, but good pilots always know what to do whichever one blows their way.

THE GOOD WIND

Ever wonder why sometimes your flight arrives at your destination earlier than expected? It is usually a pleasant surprise — unless of course your welcoming party is not there yet! Well, the reason for this is that wind has been blowing your plane from the back. This is what we call a strong tailwind, a boost, as if someone is pushing you to make you move faster.

Wind can be good, bad or ugly depending on how it is perceived in relation to the plane. Wind is good when it helps to speed up a long journey, but bad when it is blowing the plane from the back during a landing. Tailwind can cause the landing distance to be longer, thus reducing the safety margin. Sometimes, it may even cause a tailstrike in which the bottom of the aircraft scrapes the runway.

Similarly, it is good when the wind is blowing from the front on take-off or landing and hence a shorter runway is required, but bad on a long flight as it takes a longer time to reach your destination.

On take-off, a strong headwind gets the plane airborne faster compared with a tailwind. As such, the air traffic controller will use a runway with the strongest headwind.

Consequently, some delays are to be expected when there is a need to change runway owing to a shift in wind direction, for safety reasons. All planes have to be resequenced either on the ground or in the air.

CROSSWIND LANDINGS

Wind can be ugly when it blows across the runway at speeds beyond the limitations imposed by the manufacturer. This is known as crosswind.

For instance, on an Airbus A330, when wind exceeds 40 knots, landing is not allowed on a dry runway. If the

Making a crosswind landing.

runway is wet and slippery, the crosswind limit is reduced to 27 knots as it is more difficult to keep the plane centred on a slippery runway.

On Aug 22, 1999, a China Airlines McDonnell Douglas MD-11 flight to Hong Kong crashed because of strong crosswinds. Strong crosswind landings may be a little difficult as the nose is pointed to the crosswind direction in order to maintain the centre line of the runway. It looks awkward as the plane has to "crab in" and only points the nose back to the runway centre line just before touching down.

In the Hong Kong accident, the captain landed hard on the right landing gear. As a result, the right engine scraped the runway, causing the right main landing gear and the wing on that side to break off. The plane then rolled inverted as it skidded off the runway.

There are lessons to be learned by pilots. Never land or take off when the crosswind is beyond the manufacturer's recommended limitations.

TRYST WITH A TYPHOON

I vividly remember an incident some years back in Shanghai when I was working for my former airline. I refused to take off on a Boeing 777 because of an approaching typhoon. An irate passenger said something to this effect: "How come the other airline's Boeing 777 pilot was able to take off while this cowardly pilot refuses to?" This remark prompted the airport manager to try and persuade me to take off. I adamantly told him, "No way, my friend!"

I, too, was surprised that the Boeing 777 parked next to us had taken off. Of course, this angered the passengers who had been stranded at the lounge for several hours. It made plain sense to them: If the other flight could take off, then why was this pilot (yours truly) being difficult?

I had my reasons, and good ones they were too. You see, an approaching typhoon comes with winds that gradually increase in strength. Worse still, the wind on that day was blowing across the runway. Every plane has a crosswind limitation beyond which the manufacturer cannot guarantee a safe take-off.

The wind on that fateful day was gusting well above the take-off limit, hence my refusal to take off and endanger the lives of those in my care.

An approaching typhoon.

NO WAY, JOSÉ!

I tried my best to explain the reasons behind my refusal to take off but the airport manager was not convinced. However, that all changed when we heard over the radio that a United Airlines Boeing 747 and a Virgin Atlantic Airbus A340 were forced to return after aborting their departures. I was pleased that I had stood firm in refusing to give in to the demands of the airline's airport manager. My passengers' safety was of the utmost importance and I was certainly not about to take a chance on it. I recalled a doctor's comment once about my responsibility being heavier than his. He remarked that when a doctor makes a mistake, only one patient dies, whereas a pilot's mistake would impact the lives of over 300 passengers!

The other pilot might have been trying to be heroic but each time we pilots sign in to fly an aircraft, we are duty-bound — morally and professionally — to fly as safely as possible. In all honesty in this instance, I would rather be a coward who is alive (along with all his passengers) than a dead hero!

HANDLING WIND SHEAR

A recent report alleged that wind shear was the probable cause of a Boeing 737 crashing into the sea at Bali International Airport in 2013. Fortunately, all 101 passengers and seven crew survived the crash even after the plane broke apart in shallow waters.

"Err, maybe the Captain was right after all..."

Severe wind shear can be very vicious. It is caused by a sudden and powerful change in wind direction that occurs frequently in or near thunderstorms. The downdraft created can give rise to a strong headwind that will cause a corresponding increase in airspeed. When a plane passes through the downdraft, it encounters a tailwind, which will cause the aircraft to dangerously lose airspeed and altitude.

Airplanes are most vulnerable to wind shear during take-offs and landings, and the situation can turn very ugly should pilots be caught by surprise. It has also caused several crashes.

On June 24, 1975, an Eastern Air Lines Boeing 727 crashed while landing at the JFK International Airport owing to severe wind shear caused by thunderstorms. Of the 124 people on board, 106 passengers and six crew members did not make it. The investigation board found that the captain was aware of severe wind shear reports on the approach path but decided to continue nonetheless. That was a fatal decision.

On Aug 7, 1975, a Continental Airlines Boeing 727 crashed after take-off from the International Airport at Denver, Colorado because of severe wind shear. One hundred and thirty-four people aboard the aircraft survived the crash, with 15 persons seriously injured. The aircraft was badly damaged.

On July 9, 1982, a Pan American World Airways Boeing 727 flight crashed on take-off after encountering wind shear. The aircraft was destroyed during the impact and subsequent ground fire and there were many fatalities.

PREDICTIONS AND WARNINGS

Lest all these accidents worry you, improvements in technology have come to the rescue. Human beings are very innovative. Lessons from past incidents always help to make flying safer for the future.

Today, wind shear-detection technology has been developed to enable pilots to predict any change in wind speed and direction even before take-off. Most modern planes, including the Airbus A320 and A330, are now installed with this technology.

Basically, this warning system makes use of the weather radar to identify the existence of wind shear before take-off. The radar picks up water and ice particles ahead of the airplane and warns the pilot with this audio message: "Wind Shear Ahead!" This is effective and provides the pilot an opportunity to abort the take-off.

While airborne or during take-off and landing, this system also warns of any wind shear ahead. It is not clear whether the wind shear warning was activated in the Boeing 737 accident in Bali when the wind conditions subsided.

LORD OF THE WINDS

The next time you see a plane landing cocked (pointing) towards the wind and not on the runway centre line, you will know that the captain is working very hard to control a crosswind landing. He has to do that "crabbing" or else he will miss aligning on the runway centre line. Not to worry. Just before touchdown, he will use the rudder to point the plane back towards the centre. Intensive wind shear practices by pilots in AirAsia include a mandatory twice-yearly check to ensure that our passengers are safely taken care of at all times.

With that in mind, I hope to relieve any anxieties you may have as a result of gusty winds during your future flights.

DOWN MEMORY LANE

I started my flying lessons on the Chipmunk plane in 1967.

Image by Joop de Groot

This Chipmunk (WG 486) which I flew at my flying school, RAF Church Fenton, UK, is still flying, mainly for historical display.

I then progressed to advanced flying on the Jet Provost.

I flew this Jet Provost at RAF Acklington, UK in 1968.

My last flight on the Boeing 777 from Cairo to Kuala Lumpur in March 2006.

In April 2006, I retired from Malaysia Airlines and joined AirAsia to fly the Airbus 320.

In 2009, I was flying the Airbus 330 with AirAsia X.

My favourite four-engine plane, the Airbus A340, which I flew with AirAsia X.

Jinda Bisran (centre) dispatching my last flight out of London Stansted.

My last flight from London on the Airbus A340 in March 2011.

Saying farewell to my flying colleagues and Allstars of AirAsia X in March 2011.

The cabin crew who operated with me, prior to a flight.

Meet a set of great cabin crew.

Tony Fernandes with a copy of Life in the Skies.

The launch of my first book, Life in the Skies, by Aireen Omar and Tony Fernandes in 2013.

Life in the Skies was placed third in the POPULAR-The Star Readers' Choice Awards at BookFest @ Malaysia 2015.

Book signing after the launch of Life in the Skies.

Launch of the Chinese version of Life in the Skies by Tony Fernandes in 2015.

I was invited to TEDx Talks by TEDxPetaling Street in 2015.

At the end of my TEDx Talk on 'All About Flying'.

Promoting the Chinese edition of Life in the Skies.

Book signing with Tony - Life in the Skies (Chinese version) - at the Kuala Lumpur Convention Centre in 2015.

Pre-flight briefing prior to A330 flight simulator training.

Operating as an Airbus A330 flight simulator instructor after retiring from flying.

The interior of an Airbus A320 flight simulator where I conduct the pilot training.

ABOUT THE AUTHOR

Captain Lim Khoy Hing is an ex-airline pilot. Prior to his retirement from the airlines, he flew all the latest fly-by-wire planes such as the Boeing 777 and Airbus A320, A330 and A340. He has logged a total of 25,500 flying hours.

Captain Lim was trained by the RAF in the United Kingdom in 1967. He served with the Royal Malaysian Air Force for about 13 years prior to joining Malaysian Airline System Berhad (now known as Malaysia Airlines Berhad).

In 2006, he flew with another airline, AirAsia, then AirAsia X until 2011, when he retired at the age of 65. He is now a flight simulator instructor with AirAsia X. Occasionally, he also trains airline pilots at the Asian Aviation Centre of Excellence.

Captain Lim pursued his law studies as an external student of the University of London while he was with the airlines. He has an LLB (Hons)(London) degree and a Malaysian Certificate of Legal Practice, but is not a practicing lawyer.

Captain Lim is happily married with a son (engineer), who lives in Kuala Lumpur, and a daughter (IT consultant), who lives in London. He has five grandchildren.

ABOUT THE AUTHOR

Captain Lim and his family.

His first book, *Life in the Skies*, was published in 2013. It has since become a regional bestseller and won third prize in the POPULAR–*The Star* Readers' Choice Awards at Bookfest @ Malaysia, in 2015.

He now spends his time with his grandchildren, occasionally writing articles for *Travel 3Sixty* magazine and running his website at www.askcaptainlim.com for the benefit of aspiring pilots and fearful flyers. He can be contacted via his website.